VERA DUCKWORTH

My Story

BLAKE

Published by Blake Publishing Ltd,
98–100 Great North Road, London N2 0NL, England

First published in Great Britain in 1993

ISBN 185782 0436

British Library Cataloguing-in-Publication Data: A catalogue
record for this book is available from the British Library.

Typeset by MFK Typesetting Ltd., Hitchin, Herts

Printed and bound in Great Britain by BPCC Paperbacks Ltd

13579108642

To my family, and to my friend Jack.

Contents

Introduction

I don't think anything can begin to prepare you for *Coronation Street*. It's nearly 20 years since I first walked into the most famous address in the land, and sometimes I feel as though my feet have never touched the ground since. All at the same time it is wonderful and terrifying, exhilarating and exhausting, happy and sometimes sad.

It has taken me, an ordinary working-class mother of four who sang a bit in the northern clubs to pay for a few extras for the kids, to meet the Queen, to hit some horrifying headlines, to be featured on *This Is Your Life*, and to be welcomed into millions of people's homes three times a week.

All the way along that amazing journey I have hardly been able to take in that this was happening to me. The *Coronation Street* stars were my heroes and heroines as I grew up in Leeds. I once paid out my last half crown and queued for hours and hours just to sit on Dennis Tanner's knee.

Never, ever in my wildest dreams did I imagine that one day people would stand in line to meet me, that Her Majesty the Queen would discuss Mike Baldwin's factory with me, that my private indiscretions would be paraded and exaggerated in screaming headlines or that I would meet some of the world's most talented and famous stars.

Coronation Street is an institution. I have always known that, but many times during those 20 years I have wondered whether all the pressures and stresses of working on the show would see me finish up in a very different sort of institution. I love the show with all my heart and I admire and respect all the people who work on it. But it's not easy at times. The standard of the show demands the best of everyone involved, and in my opinion that's why it's the tops.

I've made mistakes along the way, plenty of them. But I try to look forward and I never try too hard to change because deep down inside I know that it's the Vera they saw in me all those years ago that was my stepping stone into this fantasy land called fame.

The many letters I get from *Coronation Street* fans asking me about my life before the show and a million other questions prompted me to start writing this book. People want to know if we all get on in the Street, who are my favourite characters, where I was born, what did I do before *Coronation Street*.

What I still find funny is the way everyone talks to me as though I really am Vera. They say, 'How's your Jack? When are you going to get him some new glasses? Who's looking after Tommy? Leave Des Barnes alone!' It's real to them, and sometimes it's real to me as well.

It's a fantastic experience living large chunks of your life in the nation's front rooms three times a week. It has taken over my life and the lives of my children and my husband. It has affected us all. Sometimes I have felt

I couldn't go on, but the truth is that I love *Coronation Street* too much to want to leave. I wouldn't change a thing. I just wanted this chance to tell you what it's felt like from this side of the screen.

1
A Wartime Childhood

I know it sounds like something Vera Duckworth might come out with, but I honestly believe I can remember being born. When I mentioned it my mother used to say, 'Don't be so silly,' but as a little girl it just seemed so vivid. I used to say, 'I can remember, I can.' I could remember everything being completely dark and then a cry and then it being light, and she would say, 'Don't tell anyone. They'll think you're mad.' So I kept quiet and right up until I was six it was a really strong memory with me that felt very strange.

I made it in the end as an actress, but it took me an awful long time before I was first paid for play acting even though I did start very early in life. I simply hated the idea of sitting in class when I could be at home playing. On the way to school as a reluctant youngster my poor big brother Albert, who was reluctantly in charge of getting me there on time, had a hard task. I used to really play him up by pulling down my knickers to make him late.

There was a big piece of waste ground in between our home in Torre Mount, Leeds, and our school, and that was where I used to dawdle to a stop. I was three when I first went to school. You were allowed to start early in those days. It was a sort of nursery school that I attended at first, and I never liked the walk.

There always seemed to be dead cats lying around. I think that is one of the reasons why I don't like cats today. We were near a main road, I suppose that was it. But they had their eyes open. Ugh! It makes me shudder even now. I would take as long as possible to get to school and delay things as much as I could by pretending my knickers were coming down. I would just stop and then pull them down myself before crying plaintively to Albert: 'My knickers are coming down!'

He would have to stop and get me sorted out, and that often made him late and he would get into trouble. At one point when I was particularly naughty at making him late he got the cane every day for a week. That little game worked until a neighbour saw my trick in action one day and felt sorry for Albert. She told my mother. When she saw what I was up to the game was really up. I got a sharp crack and I never dawdled again. Today that is one of Albert's party pieces, he really loves to tell that story.

Everyone knows lots of people who think that they had the best mum and dad in the world, but it was really true for me. I was born at home, at 24 Torre Mount, on 8 November 1939. I didn't know at the time, of course, but it was just two months after the outbreak of the Second World War. Not that the War was allowed to upset my young life at all. My mother would never have permitted that. But my dad was away in the army, and times were tough for us like everyone else.

If you think I'm an actress you should have met my mother. She was a fantastic woman, there wasn't anything she couldn't do. There was no role she couldn't play brilliantly. She worked in a clothing factory that was much more of a sweatshop than Mike Baldwin's ever was, even though there were some distinct similarities. She used to keep three giant Hoffman presses going single-handed and then come home and make sure my dad and the rest of us were happy.

All I can remember from my very earliest days is laughter. I never realised it at the time, but we didn't have a lot of money, yet that never stopped us enjoying ourselves. There was always singing and music in the house and lots of larking about and it always revolved around my mother. My father would sing but my mother couldn't sing for toffee. She would be clowning around.

The most upsetting moment of our War came when the authorities came up with the frightening idea of interning my mother. Because of her dark complexion and long dark hair some bright spark thought she might have Italian blood in her and be a security threat. We laughed about it later, but I don't think it was very funny at the time.

The police came to the door in the large and frightening shape of one Detective Sergeant Onions who thoughtfully suggested that my mother might have to be interned. She wasn't Italian, of course, and it quickly came to nothing, but my father still exploded with anger when he came home on leave. 'Sgt ★★★★★ Onions,' he shouted. 'I'll go down to the police station and sort him out.'

My mother made light of it afterwards. She loved to laugh, but sometimes there was a sad side to her. When things really got her down she would sit by the fire and have a quiet cry. She did her best to hide any problems from us, but just occasionally money troubles or some other problem would get her down.

When my dad was on leave my mum and dad went down to The Eagle at the end of our road and we used to go next door for Mrs Dickinson to look after us. There was a radio programme we used to listen to called *Appointment With Fear*, presented by the Man in Black. That used to frighten us to death.

My mother was tall, which must be where I get my height from. My dad was about average height, I suppose, but he was very good looking. I always think he looked like John Mills. He used to love to go fishing, and to read Western novels. I think he always secretly thought he was John Wayne.

He was good at sports. He played semi-professional football and cricket, and he was very good at snooker and all the pub games like darts and dominoes as well. He used to love to keep fit when he was younger. Sometimes he would do these stretching exercises, going down on just one knee and rising up again to keep his body supple, and he would get all of us doing them with him. We must have looked as though we were mad if anyone had gone by.

I suppose my mother used to shield me from a lot of

the hardship because I can't remember us ever being short of anything. We didn't have a car, but nobody else had a car either so that didn't matter. Everybody had a job of some sort and everybody seemed to rub along and make some sort of a living. We didn't meet any rich people, of course. We just didn't come into contact with any million-aire millowners or whatever in those days.

When I was just a little bump in my mother's stomach a friend took her and my dad racing. At the meeting, in the summer of 1939, there was a caravan with a gypsy fortune teller who solemnly predicted to them: 'You will have a daughter and she will be as fair as a lily. You will call her Sylvia and she will never want.'

My mother never thought a lot more about it until I was born, and I came into the world almost perfectly white. I was nearly an albino. Then when the family were choos-ing names for me they just couldn't agree. My father wanted to call me one thing while an auntie suggested an-other and my uncle said I looked just like someone else.

My mother put all the names into a hat. When she picked one out, it was Sylvia. My real name is Sylvia But-terfield. My mother remembered the gypsy's prediction then and hoped the third part about never wanting for any-thing would come true as well. Eventually it did, but that would be getting ahead of myself.

Our home was an ordinary working-class council house, not back-to-back like Coronation Street, but a semi-detached with a garden out front and another at the back. There were three bedrooms upstairs and the living room and the kitchen downstairs. I was born in that front room, in a bed brought downstairs. It's not what you've got in life that matters but how much love you have in your life. And I had plenty from the start.

If we didn't look after our clothes we were in trouble. My mum always made sure we were well dressed, even though we bought most of our things on 'tick' from a woman that came round. We paid it off weekly – everybody lived like that in those days. Cash was always in short supply. Poor Albert had a pair of brand new boots that landed him in deep trouble. Just after he got them he went out and they were playing jumping over the beck. Unfortunately for Albert, he tried one of the wider sections and landed right in the middle, soaking and spoiling his new boots. He cried his eyes out and didn't want to go home. When he did eventually come back he got into real trouble. He'd only had them about a week and the boots were ruined.

He had even less luck when he got a toy machine gun for Christmas. Dad had made a replica of a sten gun for him and it was very lifelike. It had a ratchet inside to make that authentic rat-a-tat-tat sound. Albert was really made up with it. But the police took it off him. They said it was just too realistic. I think they must have thought he was going to declare war on Lancashire.

My mother always wanted us to have all the things she'd never had as a girl, so she worked herself very, very hard. When I was about three years old she was pregnant and had to give up her job in the clothing factory. But she went straight to another job in the fish and chip shop on nearby Hillcrest Road.

It was terrible, back-breaking work peeling pounds and pounds of potatoes in freezing cold water. We must have needed the money, but when my dad came home on leave from the army he put a stop to that. She was expecting twins and the work was much too strenuous.

My mother duly had the twins – a boy and a girl – but tragically they did not live very long. I can just dimly remember all the hushed family conferences that heralded a dreadful event.

My brother Albert took me out in East End Park with his friends; they must have told him to take me out of the way. To attract attention I kept saying that I had fallen, and at first they would come rushing but they gradually took less and less notice of me.

So when I did actually fall and cut my leg on a nasty piece of wire nobody came. Eventually, when they realised it was serious, one of my brother's friends had to carry me home on his back. While we'd been away my mother had had the babies. My father had to take me to have my foot stitched. Poor father, every time he came home on leave there was something.

The twins were born at home but they arrived very prematurely. We didn't have a cot. They just used drawers out of the sideboard to put the babies in. But very soon they took one into hospital, a little boy called Michael, and sadly he did not survive long.

The policeman came and grimly told us that he had to

inform us that the baby in hospital had died. And then when my father was breaking the awful news to my mother he realised the other twin, Mary, was dead as well. She had just passed peacefully away in my mother's arms. It must have been absolutely heartbreaking for both of them.

My father went out and my grandmother came and took the baby gently away. It must have been traumatic, and they would rarely talk about it afterwards. I was four then, so I can only barely remember. It was such a dreadful thing for my mother to cope with, and yet she protected us from it.

I remember how my mother cried after that. She was absolutely heartbroken. The family rallied round and helped, and my dad came home on compassionate leave for about a week. That was as much compassion as the British Army could muster. It didn't seem long to grieve for two lost children.

My father didn't have to go in the Army because he was an engineer, which was a reserved occupation, but one or two lads from our street got killed. Until then my dad had been in the Home Guard. They used to train in East End Park, charging with bayonets at these bags standing in for German soldiers. But my dad felt a bit guilty being out of the fighting after people we knew had died, so he joined up. I think he got it into his head that people were pointing at him a bit, saying that he was using his reserved occupation to keep out of the fighting, and he wasn't having that. He came out and volunteered.

But he went straight from his engineering factory to

an armaments plant. He was sent down to High Wycombe, and while he was there he played football for Wycombe Wanderers. Later he worked on the preparations for D-Day, waterproofing all the vehicles that were to be used in the invasion across the English Channel. It was a massive job. He used to say that they travelled 11 miles as they went from vehicle to vehicle. There were that many tanks and armoured cars to deal with.

My father was a skilled engineer and at first he worked for Adamson's, a big engineering factory in Leeds while my mother worked for Summeries on her presses. She worked so hard she used to sweat buckets. I swear the metal stays in her corsets used to go green.

During the War my mother used to go to this wood-yard for logs to burn on our fire, and on one visit the man in charge said she couldn't have any wood because his mate who operated the other end of the two-man saw had not turned up for work that day. 'I'll do it,' said my mother, and at first he thought she was joking. But she was deadly serious. We needed warmth in our house and she got on the end of that saw and we got that load of logs for free for once.

She was a tremendously hard-working woman. After a back-breaking day's work she would come home and start decorating. She was always very house proud. She always seemed to be wallpapering or painting one room or another. My father would say, 'Leave it as it is, woman, it's all right,' but she wouldn't listen. She wanted everything to be just as good as it could be. If it meant distempering until four o'clock in the morning she would get it done.

I've never known anyone work as hard as my mother. She used to have us helping to make clip rugs. We did it so often I thought it was a game, but we had the most beautiful floor-coverings as a result.

She went to a Catholic retreat for a weekend once for a well-earned rest. And when she was there at night she saw a woman come to the side of her bed and my mother said, 'Are you all right, love? Is there anything I can do for you?' because my mother would be straight into action if anyone was in trouble or needed any help. But there was no reply, and next morning just as she mentioned the incident to a friend she noticed on the wall a picture of the lady who had approached her. But she had been dead for 200 years. I think I get my belief in clairvoyance and mystical powers from my mother. I'm not a crank or anything, but I do firmly believe there are things that go on in people's minds and in the world that are outside normal understanding.

She was always so keen to provide the best she could for us. She used to belong to all these savings clubs so that we had a club cheque payout at Christmas and every year at Whitsuntide we all had new clothes.

We had enormous respect for her. I remember Albert didn't care at all if he got the cane at school, which he frequently did. But he was always very fearful that my mother should find out. None of us wanted to be the one to let her down in any way. We knew she would be upset and that would upset us even more than the physical pain of a caning.

Every time my mum was expecting a baby she would

write to my dad on a flour bag and tell him. They used flour bags as writing paper in those days. I remember standing on the outhouse roof and Albert saying, 'Me dad's here,' and I was pleased to see him, but he had a kitbag and all I was really interested in was what was in the kitbag for me.

Once he came home without us knowing – he had just got a last-minute leave. He took us all to the Odeon to see Bing Crosby in *Going My Way*. I've liked that film ever since that day.

My brother Albert is four years older than me, and my sister Maisie arrived seven years after me. During the War I was just a toddler so I can't remember the really difficult times. I think we were a bit spoilt. We had a two-week holiday every year, we always went off on a coach to Scarborough or Blackpool where the sun was somehow always shining.

We played for hours on the sands and walked on the front. My mum and dad loved each other for certain. You could tell that just from looking at them. And they also loved life. They always seemed able to get the most out of every free moment, and holiday time was precious.

Not that we kids were always perfect. Once in our boarding house in Blackpool I got down for breakfast with Albert and my mum and dad and there was no sign of our Maisie. I asked my dad where she was and he just sighed and said, 'Don't ask, just don't ask.'

I went back upstairs, and in the bedroom there were open cases strewn all over the place with clothes chucked everywhere. I said, 'Mother, you'll miss breakfast, they're waiting to clear away.'

My mother said, 'Oh, I can't . . .' and it was about the only time I ever saw her speechless. She was just dumbfounded by our Maisie, who would not wear what she was supposed to wear. Maisie was standing there in a pyjama top, a skirt, and a hairstyle that had one plait stuck out like Keyhole Kate and the rest hanging down. We had to eat our breakfast with her looking like that. And she insisted on walking up and down the promenade looking like I don't know what. She had a mind of her own, did the baby of the family.

Because my dad was away in the Army in the War it must have been very hard for my mother, managing on her own. But as well as my dad she was very much in love with Clark Gable and she consoled herself with the cinema. She used to love films. Every week we would walk off to the nearby Hillcrest Cinema and we would sit and cry our eyes out together at the most wonderful romantic films.

My mother and I both enjoyed a good cry. She was a great romantic, my mother, and I think I inherited that. The world of films seemed so glamorous, and they were always part of our life. She loved musicals, and particularly the ones starring Fred Astaire and Ginger Rogers. I always used to imagine myself as Ginger Rogers when I was a girl, but it's only now she's getting on in years that I'm afraid I'm even starting to look like her!

She and my dad even met at the cinema. She was there with a girlfriend and my dad and his pal were flicking bits of paper at them. The first time he arranged to meet my mother his trousers were too short, and he tried to cover it up by pulling them down to stretch the braces a bit. The first time my mother took him home my grandad said, 'Where do you live?' And a few days later he just turned up out of the blue at my dad's family house. He said, 'I've just come to see who my daughter is going out with.'

After the War my dad went back to his old job, and life improved for us and for everybody.

2
A Loving Family

When I was nine we moved to a new house at Halton Moor. I thought it was lovely. There was a sort of innocence around then. I don't know if it was just because I was protected, but I never felt threatened and nervous about walking round anywhere like children must do today. If we got into trouble it would usually be for something that would just be laughed off today.

I remember the police came round to our house once when Albert and some other boys had been playing on haystacks. He had been in a gang of about ten of them jumping on haystacks and flattening them. He finished up in hot water over that and got a leathering from my dad for bringing the police round. These days I don't think the police would give that sort of behaviour a second thought.

My dad loved to sing, and I think he had a lovely voice, he sounded just like Bing Crosby. He used to sing in pubs, especially when he'd had a few drinks, but mainly at home. I will always remember him singing 'Daddy's Little Girl' to me when I was sitting on his knee, and 'By the Light of the Silvery Moon' was another of my favourites. We always had a piano in the house and my mum or dad would often say, 'Come on, let's have a sing-song,' and we'd all gather round the piano.

My mother loved to hear the piano. I used to play, but not with sheet music. She did once send me for piano lessons but the theory of it all never really went into my head. If you hummed a tune I could follow it, so I think they thought I had some talent. It was half a crown a lesson, but I hated it. One day I just threw the music up into the air and ran home with the music teacher chasing me. But I can still bash a tune out today.

They were really easy-going, my parents. They believed life was for living. They used to work hard, certainly, but they knew how to enjoy themselves. Our house was always full of friends and family and the music and jokes never stopped. A lot of my friends used to say, 'Oh, I can't go out tonight. I've got to wash my hair or do my homework or whatever.' I seemed to play out all the time.

One night the girls in the street asked me to come out and play jumping over people's privet hedges. It seemed innocent and harmless enough until I jumped over this hedge and crashed into a brick wall on the other side with my face first. I had only been out for five minutes and I left half my top lip on that brick wall and I was in absolute agony. I ran in and my mother nearly fainted. I had to go to hospital and have emergency treatment.

That's where my luck came in as there was a top plastic surgeon at Jimmy's, or St James's Hospital, Leeds, to give it its official title. They took me to the local infirmary first and there they said I would be left with a hare lip and my teeth exposed if I wasn't operated on properly. This chap at St James's was the only man in Leeds who could do it right and I was fortunate that he was available. Otherwise my life might have been very different.

I can remember looking at my jagged lip in a mirror when I first got to the hospital. Everybody who came up to me and took a look sort of winced at me. So I decided to look for myself. It was a shock. It had all swollen, and my head spun. It was terrible, and after it was stitched it was all shiny and weird. The surgeon took the skin to build my new lip from my bum. I've made plenty of jokes about people kissing my bottom since then.

I think I must have been a bit accident prone as a young girl. I used to take my younger sister Maisie home, and if my mum was at work I would love to tidy up and set the table for her. Once my sister got the bread and was cutting the crust over the table after all my careful cleaning up and I just reached out and grabbed the bread knife and it nearly took my finger end right off. It was just hanging off by a thread of skin.

I ran screaming across the road to a neighbour. He had just got in from work and was still in his boiler suit and he said, 'Right, quick, I'll nip you down to the hospital on the bus to get that stitched.' I said, 'Oh no, I'll wait until my mother gets home.' It wasn't that I needed my mother – it was just that I didn't want to go with him on the bus in his boiler suit.

It's awful how you only remember the shocking

things from your early childhood. I know I had loads of idyllic days just playing out in the street or inside with the family, but so many memories become blurred with the passing of time.

One of the biggest frights I ever had as a young girl was when someone threw a cat onto my back. I was absolutely terrified and to this day I have never liked being near cats. I was just playing in the street outside our house and for a joke this cat was chucked onto my back. I was wearing a woolly cardigan and it just clung on to that, and through that to my skin. I swung round and it still clung on, I couldn't shake it off. The poor creature was probably just as frightened as I was but ever since then I have found cats a bit creepy.

My mother and dad had their ups and downs like any couple, but they never let the kids see if there was any real trouble. They did have their silences when there had been a difference of opinion, though. They were hilarious. We used to be passing messages backwards and forwards when they weren't talking to each other. It was all, 'Dad, my mum says your tea is ready.'

It was really funny when they had a difference of opinion over something. My dad used to do the silent treatment. My mother would be ranting and raving fit to bust. My dad would just sit there as though it didn't bother him at all, but I knew it did really. He just had this control and he could go really calm and I would be thinking, 'I wish my dad would say something. Why doesn't my dad say something?' because I knew once he said something it would all be over. Everything revolved round your dad in those days, and he must have been a very clever man. He was always making the most amazing inventions around the house, and building tool-boxes.

But sometimes his patience would snap and he would bang his pot down hard on the table and say, 'That's enough!' and my mother would go all quiet and weepy for a while. Then she would have a little pretend cry and go all coy, and it would all be forgotten and they would be laughing again. But during the silences, if anyone came to the door she used to say all brightly as though nothing at all was wrong, 'Oh, hello. Do come in!'

In those days handling the family budget was a work of art. When my dad came home from work on pay day he would hand over his pay packet to my mum and she would do all the managing. She would give him so much and then she did all the paying out. She looked after him really well.

My mum was the second oldest of her family but her older brother went away to the Navy so she had a big hand in bringing all her younger brothers and sisters up. She was fiercely protective, just like she was with us. 'You can say what you like but they're mine,' she used to say. It was a good feeling to be one of her brood.

They never had a car but then they only ever went to the club on the corner. My mother worked from when Maisie was six weeks old until she was dying. Whenever you went to see my mum in the tailoring factory the same women would be in the same places. There would be Nellie Platt here, Nellie Varley and her daughter Shirley ironing over there, and little Anne who was the buttoner. They were all lovely women. They stayed there for years and years. It was more than just a job, it was a way of life. They knew you and you knew them for life. They would do anything for you. They worked together all their lives and watched each other's children growing up.

In some families, like with Grandad Shaw, my mother's father, it was the man who laid down the law and made all the rules and regulations, but with us it was my mother – though if my dad really put his foot down he was always the 'ultimate' boss.

My mother had this amazing inner strength. It seemed that with her anything was possible. She was very strong and very kind, and she was a very honourable woman. If anything went wrong or somebody did something awful she would never rush in and condemn like so many people. She would just go quiet and say, 'Well, you know, they're somebody's child.' It's a lot to live up to. If someone did something really nasty she would never be nasty back, she would just say, 'Oh, they're having an off day. You don't know what's gone on. They might have dreadful trouble at home.'

Often after school I would be holding Maisie by the hand, just coming out, when we would find Father Murphy the parish priest looming up. He was well over six feet tall with a shock of white hair, and he looked quite a frightening figure with his long black coat on. He would say, 'Now come along, Sylvia, I want you to sing for me.' And we would go off into the church hall and I would be pushed onto the stage. Maisie would be right at the back of the hall and I would have to sing a hymn, just for him. It became a sort of private concert. I was always a bit reluctant, but if the priest said you were to do something you did it.

Albert was a Bevin boy, he went down the pit when he was 16 and when he was on shifts he would have to get up at about five in the morning and he would sing 'Wheel of Fortune' at the top of his voice to wake us all up. It never seemed anything but natural to us to sing, but I can remember this was going a bit too far.

People were always wanting me to sing. We used to have concerts behind the curtain and I would hide behind, perched on the window sill, and someone would have to pull the curtain back and then I would sing a song. But I was shy about it. I would forbid them all to look at me while I sang, so I'd be singing away and everybody would be looking at the wall.

Every Friday night they used to have this ritual called 'settling up'. My dad used to sit and read his paper and then he would fold it so he could write down the edge. Then he would start to make a list. He would have his pencil and he would be ages, an hour, maybe longer. He would go, 'Insurance three and sixpence . . .'

Over on the other side of the room my mother would say quietly, 'What are you doing, Albert?'

'Just adding up what you owe me,' he'd say. Eventually she would look at his list and then she would get a pencil and a piece of paper and she would go, 'Packet of Seven O'clock razor blades, newspapers four and sixpence, Woodbines seven and sixpence, pair of socks half a crown, a pound in the roll-up . . .'

It would add up to, say, £5 15 shillings and he would grumble on and on because she always seemed to come out on top. He always had to give her more money. It would all come down to a few pence they had paid the window cleaner that he was moaning about.

Those weekly accounting sessions were the source of a lot of amusement to us when we were growing up. They went on for years and when I got older I used to say to dad, 'Why do you do it? You know you'll end up owing my mother £2.' He would say, 'I know, but one day I'll get one over on her.' He would be moaning that he hadn't even wanted a new pair of socks and she would be saying, 'Well you're still paying me for them.'

I knew even as a girl that nobody would ever love me like my dad loved my mother. He used to reminisce sometimes and he would go all dreamy and say, 'There was never anyone to compare with your mother. Do you know she had a 19 inch waist when I met her. My, she was lovely.' She was the most beautiful girl in Stoney Rock.

He was really proud to be married to her. All parents have their ups and downs, but looking back the amount of love and affection in my home was phenomenal. None of us could go to sleep until we had kissed each other 'Goodnight and God bless'. That would have been unthinkable.

Before he got injured at work, my dad was a very fit bloke. He was brilliant at football and cricket and I think that was partly why I loved sport at school. He used to like a drink at the weekend, but he never went out in the week. He was happiest just sitting in his chair smoking his beloved Woodbines and reading a book in front of the fire. He could take a joke as well. Our Albert was always playing him up at mealtimes, he would say, 'Who's that coming to our house?' and then pinch a piece of meat off my dad's plate when he looked away.

What your parents are rubs off on you, so I grew up a romantic in a world where everybody lived happily ever after and men sang songs to women and then proposed.

A marriage like my parents' takes a lot of living up to, because you tend to compare your marriage with their tremendously happy one. Years later I wanted Don and me to be for our kids what my mum and dad were for me. Because it never mattered what anyone said or did to us, I would always say, 'I'll tell my mum,' and that was like the ultimate weapon. My mum was an absolute rock. It was not that my dad was weak, it was just that she was something really special, 'My Mum'.

When me moved to Halton Moor we lived next door to a miner who was on very big money. A lot of my dad's family were colliers, so I suppose it was partly in his blood. This bloke encouraged my dad to join him down the pit and I will always remember him coming home, black with coal. There were no pithead baths in those days.

That meant we were in on one of the great highlight events on our estate, when the coal came. It was one of the perks of a collier's job to get free coal. When it arrived it literally fell off the back of a lorry. A coal wagon just backed up outside the house and a great load was dumped there in the road. We kids used to rush round and help get it all in buckets. Every six weeks we had a coal delivery. It was quite exciting – all young kids like getting mucky, and I was no different.

The neighbours used to come out and help because then they would get some free coal. So we used to try to get the big bits in first, and then what was left my dad used to say, 'Help yourself.'

But he had only been a miner for six months when he was injured. A big fall of coal landed on his back and he ended up wearing a steel corset. He stopped work for a time and then went back and did only light jobs which meant that his wage packet was a lot lighter too.

I've always had a great affection for the mining industry. The recent news about pit closures really saddened me because they are proud people, miners, you know. I can remember when people used to say to girls if they went out with a collier they were sure of a good wage coming in. My grandfather has been a collier, too, so coal dust must be in my blood as well. Miners always seemed so strong and brave to me, like real-life heroes, and we all admired them.

Halton Moor used to be such a beautiful area to live in. We used to go for lovely long walks to Temple Newsam, just meandering along, a gang of us without a care in the world. We always seemed to be having long games of rounders or cricket on the green just in front of our house. Girls used to play cricket then.

I must have had my head in the clouds half the time. I can hardly ever remember feeling unhappy as a kid. We always felt so secure, so protected. I couldn't have been happier if I'd been born to a pair of millionaire parents.

My dad used to love his fishing. I suppose if you've worked all day in a factory or down a pit you are bound to want some fresh air in your free time. Sometimes he'd take one or two of us kids. We enjoyed it. He used to have us tramping for miles over fields to get to some special bit of river or lake. My mother quite liked it too. I think we must have looked like The Waltons. We'd sit on the river bank reading, but we had to be quiet or else we'd scare the fish away. My dad was in a fishing club and sometimes we'd go on fishing trips in a ramshackle old bus.

But my mother wasn't that keen on the animal world. She viewed anything on four legs with the greatest suspicion, and one rather hair-raising encounter with a bull did nothing to ease her concern.

It was on one of my dad's frequent fishing trips when he had persuaded my mother that the whole family could go along and witness his skill with a rod. But there was this large, unfriendly-looking bull in the field we had to cross. My mother kept shouting, 'Albert, are you sure it's safe?' He was trudging on ahead with all his fishing tackle over his shoulder and he just called back over his shoulder, 'Yes, there's no danger. Just follow me.'

Unfortunately my dad knew more about fish than he did about farm animals, and this bull made a beeline for us. It started to run and we ignored all my dad's confident reassurances that there was no danger and sprinted for the gate. We made it just in time. My dad really laughed.

My mother always had certain psychic powers. Sometimes she would just know what was going to happen before it happened. Once, when my dad was working down the pit, she said to the woman next door whose husband worked there as well, 'Albert won't be coming home with Chris because he has gone to the hospital and he is having stitches in his thumb.'

The neighbour said, 'Don't be silly. How would you know if he had?' My mum said she had seen the accident happen in a dream. She had awoken immediately. It was 2 a.m. Then the neighbour's husband came home and told her that my dad had hurt his thumb and gone down to get it stitched. The accident had happened at the exact time my mother had dreamed of it.

My mum just knew, and she didn't really know how she knew. Another time a woman at work had a daughter who was having a baby and it was going to be her first grandchild so naturally she was very excited. My mum told her, 'Your daughter has had a baby, a big baby, and there is something wrong with its eyes but it is nothing to worry about, it is not serious.' When the grandmother went to the hospital that night she asked the nurse about this and the nurse was amazed and just said. 'How on earth did you know that?' The facts were just as my mother had recounted.

She used to say that when she first had me as a baby she saw a nun standing over my cot calming me down and holding my hand. This nun just looked mysteriously at my mother and said, 'I knew you needed to sleep.' For years when I was growing up at night-times my brother Albert used to shout, 'Goodnight mum, goodnight dad, goodnight Sylvia. I hope she doesn't come tonight.' I used to have this awful vision of the nun coming to get me. It was horrible. I used to have nightmares for years. But I think I have had a guiding angel at my shoulder.

My mother's father, Grandad Shaw, frightened me. I remember always being scared to go to my granny's house. He used to have a big leather belt and a funny eye and I used to say to my mother before every trip, 'I'm not going,' and she just used to say, 'Don't be silly.' He had a really loud voice that didn't exactly welcome arguments from anyone and my granny made sure we behaved. We weren't allowed to speak at the table.

Looking back on it now, I realise it was a street just like Coronation Street and the loo was outside up this yard. I used to hate to have to go up there, I would rather sit cross-legged for hours and try to wait until we got home than be sent up the yard with the key. My mother would know, though, and say, 'Off you go with the key.' I don't know why but I was so frightened by that outside loo. I can't think what I imagined was going to happen to me in there, but I was scared stiff of going. It was just so awful, all sparkling clean whitewash inside, but I was afraid of something – somebody locking me in or a spider or a mouse, I'm not sure. It became a real phobia for me. Every time I heard we were going to granny's I used to think, 'Oh God. How can I avoid going to their toilet?'

It was up Stoney Rock in Leeds but has been pulled down long since. My grandfather worked with horses and he loved them. He drove a cart for a brewery. His great claim to fame was taking a horse on stage as part of a show at the Empire and then having it mess all over. He used to enter his horses for shows, and he would polish their brasses until they shone. He really frightened me, he always looked ever so stern, but our Maisie really loved him. I think he must have mellowed as he got older, although he died in his fifties.

My granny was a good laugh. I used to love to sit and listen to her tales. My favourite was the time she knocked my grandad out with a miraculous hangover cure. He didn't come round for three days! He liked a drink. He once put all the windows in at Stoney Rock pub after a row. Nobody tangled with him! She once gave him this potion called a drunkard's cure that she had sent for and it turned out to be a real knockout. He came home on the Friday night and she gave it to him and he didn't wake up until Tuesday. My granny and her friend were really worried. They didn't know if he was ever going to come round.

On the Tuesday morning he came down shaking his head saying something about not having to go into work that day because it was Saturday. She said, 'You've not been well.' He said, 'What do you mean?' and she had to tell him it wasn't Saturday at all but Tuesday. I think that frightened him a bit, but it didn't stop him drinking.

My mother came from a large family. My uncle, who died recently, was a chief petty officer on the Royal Yacht *Britannia* most of his working life, and he used to send us these amazing postcards saying 'This is me behind the Queen,' and he would be marked with a cross on a long line-up of immaculate sailors.

We never saw much of my father's family. His dad used to breed whippets and greyhounds and he was a very nice man by all accounts. Sadly, he died before I knew him. My other granny never went out for years. She became housebound, unfortunately, but she lived to be ninety.

My dad had two brothers, and one of them was called Bill. He had red hair and really blue eyes and a most disgusting talent. He always looked jolly but his amazing ability was for docking dogs' tails. He used to bite them off. With his teeth. I could never believe that anyone could do that.

So many attitudes were different then from today. My mother was a great Royalist. We weren't even allowed to refer to members of the Royal Family by their first names in our house as she felt it was disrespectful. I shudder to think what she would make of all the recent goings-on.

Some attitudes might seem old fashioned these days. But I'm always saddened when I go back to see the house where I spent my childhood. We used to go out and pick up all the litter and really look after the area, but these days there's rubbish everywhere and it all looks grim and unhappy. Yet every trip brings back memories.

It's funny, but when you are brought up a Catholic you are taught to believe everybody is good and in comradeship and that you can always trust your friends. My dad was not a Catholic, but my mum used to make us go to church every Sunday without fail.

The weirdest thing that happened to me was when I was about thirteen and my mother was on at me to go to church. She kept saying, 'If you don't go to confession you can't go to Mass tomorrow,' and she went on and on about it. I kept saying I didn't want to go, but she made me in the end. I ran down the hill from our house in Halton Moor and into the church. It was twenty-five minutes past six and the last confession was at half-past. I was just in time. Churches can be very spooky places, they echo so you can hear every sound.

I remember going in and I knelt down and I knew there was somebody in the confessional. It was really creepy because when I looked up there was suddenly a woman who had come out of nowhere about six pews down. She looked straight at me and slowly smiled and I thought, 'Where on earth did she come from?' because I should definitely have heard the sound of her footsteps.

Then as quickly as she had appeared she disappeared. Suddenly she was just not there. I was absolutely terrified. I rushed out and ran as fast as I could all the way home and said, 'I've just seen a ghost in church.' My mother was kind. She just sat me down and talked gently to me. It was so weird, it really freaked me out.

Later we moved again, this time to nearby Swarcliffe, right on the edge of the city. There was woodland stretching as far as the eye could see. There were no buses right to the estate – we just had to get the Barwick bus and then walk.

It was winter when we moved, and I remember us trudging over in thick snow, crunching along in our wellies, to this new house. It was a complete blanket of snow with just the hedgerows and the old street lamps showing. With the lights twinkling against the snow it looked wonderful. It was quite magical. We all got off the bus and little Maisie, who was only three then, looked up at me and said, 'Where are we?' I said, 'This is where we live now. It's Fairyland,' and for quite a while she believed me. It was amazing, though. When you have always lived surrounded by houses, to find yourself near a wood and real countryside is quite something. I suppose it *was* Fairyland. I told Maisie, 'Don't talk so loud, we don't know anyone here.'

Poor Maisie was often on the wrong end of a joke. If ever I was doing fried eggs for us and I broke one I would say, 'Oh Maisie, I'm ever so sorry, I've broken your egg,' and she never asked me why it was never my egg that got broken. For years she thought it had my name on the eggshell.

After the War we used to have a holiday every year and we would always have a completely new outfit of clothes to go in. My mother saw to that. We would go often on the bus to Scarborough, Blackpool or Bridling-ton, and I would love it. I didn't see the sea until I was seven years old, but after that we would always go and have two weeks in a boarding house.

It's a fact that we never had a lot of money but I can never remember being denied anything I really wanted, apart from one time. When *The Wizard of Oz* came on at the cinema I was bursting to go and see it. We had talked about nothing else at school. But at home the answer to all my pleas was No. I can recall swinging on our gate and sobbing my eyes out because I couldn't go. It seemed like everyone else in the world was going to this film apart from me. My mum was upset too, because she simply didn't have the entrance money to give me. But I didn't know or understand that at the time.

At Christmas we never hung up a stocking, always a pillow case. And in the morning there would be an apple, an orange and some home-made toy my father had put together. But you don't miss what you don't have. The first time I ever saw a banana was when a boy whose brother had been out in Burma brought one home. The teacher peeled it in front of us to show us this weird fruit. I thought it was very strange.

Maisie and I used to sleep together when we were little and we would always turn together in the night. We used to sleep on our sides facing the same way and there was a signal when I kicked her and we would both turn over at the same time. I always had my arm around her.

We were very close, Maisie and I. Once I had to take her to the dentist. When we got there the dentist said she would have to have a brace on her teeth, because although they were scissor straight the bottom set over-hung the top set a little. So off we went to a big dental place in Great John Street in the centre of Leeds, right next to the Museum. It was a bit novel to get a brace and after that I used to take her regularly to this place for check-ups.

I always used to say to her on the way there, 'Shall we go into the Museum?' and Maisie would say, 'I don't want to.' But I would take her anyway because they had the biggest stuffed gorilla that I had ever seen. It was a huge thing, crouched as if it would jump out. I used to tell her to look at something else and then I'd go and hide behind this big stuffed gorilla and call out, 'Maisie!' and growl like a monster. Poor Maisie would burst into tears, and when we got home she would say, 'Mum, I don't want to go back to have my teeth done there because they have this great monster that frightens me.' She was too small to explain it properly. My mother was baffled. She never did understand why there was a

monster at the dental hospital. Sometimes I look back
and think I was rather cruel to my poor little sister, but I
always came out from behind the gorilla when she got
frightened.

3
School, Boys – and Trouble

My first school was St Patrick's. It has been pulled down now, but later I went to Corpus Christi. When I was fourteen and a half I got into trouble with the senior mistress. In those days they thought nothing of giving you a smack round the head, and one day I put up my arm to protect myself. For this I was banished from classes and had to clean the headmaster's study. It was all wood, parquet flooring and a beautiful teak desk. The headmaster was called Joe Rossiter. I must have been a bit of a one because when he went out I used to barricade all the furniture behind the door and have a cigarette, blowing the smoke out of the window. He would be outside, insisting 'Let me in.' I would call out, 'I'm just polishing the floor, Mr Rossiter. You'll spoil the shine,' and he had to wait outside in the corridor until I told him it was dry.

I was very independent at school, and strong willed. I hated boring school work – so much so that when our Maisie arrived the first question she was asked by her form mistress was, 'Have you got a sister called Sylvia?' When the teacher found out she had, the next remark was, 'Well, I hope you're nothing like her.' She wasn't, as it happened – she liked school work and got prizes for it.

I think I have always been a bit contrary. My dad used to say, 'If you want our Sylvia to do something, don't ask her directly. You have to talk nicely to her and praise her a bit, then she'll run herself into the ground for you.'

The one thing I did like about school was playing netball. Being tall, I had a head start on a lot of the other girls, and I was very pleased because at last I had found something I could shine at. I remember my proudest moment at Corpus Christi came when the headmaster called me to stand out from the other girls and gravely announced: 'This is a great honour for our school. One of our girls, Sylvia Butterfield, has been chosen for the netball trials for Leeds City Girls. Well done, Sylvia.'

And everyone clapped. I went bright red as usual and bowed my head shyly, but I was very excited inside. I wasn't so proud when we got to the trial, though. It started off all right, but I just touched this other girl and she went flying. They brought me off. I was devastated. I probably was a bit tough but I was trying to do my best. And that was the high point of my netball career.

I was just too eager, I think. To be honest I knocked more than one other girl over, I bowled three or four over – I was a big girl. I just went for the ball and suddenly it was like World War Three. They were all laid there in a pile on the floor. But if I had been a footballer I would have been booked and given at least another chance. As it was I just blew my big chance. When I wanted the ball I didn't care who was in the way. My teacher fell about laughing. She thought it was a huge joke. That was a big help. But I took after my dad in that way.

Anne Harrison and Doreen Hudson were two of my best friends at school, and we got into a real scrape the time we decided to go off for a day in York. Doreen had been before and had met a really nice boy. She was keen to repeat the experience, and Anne and I were happy to go along. It was quite an experience. We were very naive, really.

We were about fourteen and the first place we went was into a pub. We all looked older than our real ages so nobody said anything. Then this local girl fell out with Doreen. She reckoned Doreen was looking at this lad that she was going out with and she started pushing Doreen in the ladies and telling her to keep off her boyfriend.

I was the biggest so I took it into my head to stick up for Doreen. I stepped forward in real Vera Duckworth style and said to this girl, 'You leave her alone.' I didn't get the chance to say anything else because she knocked me flying backwards into a rock-hard toilet seat. The next thing I knew I had the biggest bruise you've ever seen on the back of my head.

Somehow we managed to get out of the pub without getting into any more trouble, but by the time we had sorted ourselves out we had missed the bus. We had to get a taxi all the way home, which cost what seemed an absolute fortune, and my mother, bless her, paid the bill. She was so pleased to see me all in one piece she didn't even have time to be angry. She just impressed on me never, ever, to go anywhere like that again. And I never did.

Then Anne and I got into trouble for playing truant. I used to call for her on my way to school and her father was very strict. Just one look from him and you really shivered. One day we were sat listening to the radio and just decided we wouldn't go to school that day. We went off for a walk instead. We filled in notes for each other. I would say she had a cold and she would say I had laryngitis. We got away with it and we rather liked this freedom. So we had a week off. Then a bit more than a week.

But after that the 'board man', the dreaded school attendance officer, called at our house. I shook with fear. I was terrified. Anne was at our house and my mother said, 'I'm very upset with you two. I can't believe you could behave like this.' And Anne shook in her shoes.

I started crying as the board man came in, but he took one look at my dad and said, 'Hello, Albert. How are you?' They were old friends from way back, and they finished up talking away in the front room and they forgot all about me and Anne.

I hated school, I am not afraid to say. I quite liked writing and I didn't mind reading, but that was about it. Unless it was anything to do with sports I just hated it. I simply found school so boring.

All the same, it was a happy way to be brought up, on the whole. I always felt safe wherever I went. We girls knew that when you went out any of the lads from school would protect you if anything happened. But I didn't like the nuns. At Monday morning art school they would ask us if everybody had been to Mass. Most people lied if they hadn't been, but I remember once I admitted that I had not been to church because I thought it was a sin to lie and I wanted to tell them the truth. They pulled me out by the hair and I got the cane. That certainly put me right off owning up and telling the truth. I thought, I will never own up to anything again, never.

There was one thing that bothered me in my early schooldays, and that was having to stay at school for dinner. I really envied kids who went home for their dinners. My mum was working so we couldn't come home, but she listened to my moans and once she did arrange for Albert and me to go to this woman's house for our dinner. Unfortunately, the woman had a glass eye, poor soul. We could never eat the stew she cooked for us because this eye was always looking at us and we couldn't stop staring at it. She must have thought we didn't like her stew, but it wasn't that, it was just that we were transfixed by her glass eye. So we went back on school dinners again – even that was better than having the evil eye on us.

As a girl I was always very tall and thin. I was the tallest in the school I think and I always did well in the high jump. But when it came to lessons I was hopeless. I didn't even like sewing. I started a dress when I was twelve and they only made me finish it when I was leaving school. Naturally by then it was miles too short, but it shows how slow I was when it came to dressmaking.

But I did like singing, and gradually I came to realise I had quite a good voice even though I never had any real confidence. I enjoyed singing at Mass and once I went to sing for Leeds City Girls but then I was shy and I just opened my mouth and pretended to sing. I never thought for a minute I would have the nerve to stand up on stage and have people staring at me.

A friend called Marie Clariol and I did arrange to go down to auditions for the Carol Levis Show, which used to go all over the country. We must have been eleven or maybe twelve. But the night before we had been on an apple scrumping escapade in a doctor's garden near where we lived. He had loads of apples in this huge orchard and all us kids were swinging in the trees and stuffing loads of apples inside our clothes, anywhere they would stick. I had apples all over my body, up my knickers, down my socks as well as every pocket full to bursting.

Suddenly the doctor's door opened and everybody ran for it – everybody but me, that is. For some reason I froze, and he walked quickly towards me and grabbed me and pushed me up against a tree and all the apples were bouncing out of my clothes and I was terrified. He held on to me for what seemed like forever and he had hold of my throat and he just said, 'If you ever come back into my orchard again, I'll kill you.' Then he let me go and I fell on the floor and ran, clearing a four-foot barred gate with one leap.

The next day my throat was so sore I could hardly

speak. At the audition Marie sang 'This Is My Lovely Day'. Eventually I tried to croak through the Jimmy Young song, 'They Tried To Tell Us We're Too Young'.

If you got to sing all the way through it was good because usually they cut you off. And I managed to sing all the way through and I thought I was going to get a chance on the actual show. But this bloke came up afterwards and said, 'You have put your age down as fifteen but you have really got three or four years to go before that. Come back when you are older.' I was disappointed but all I could really think was, 'How did I sing with that throat?'

I didn't dream of being a singer like lots of children do, but I did know I could sing. I used to imagine myself one day grown up as a dancer. There was this elegant marble entrance in Leeds that people pretended to me was the entrance to a super dancing school. I used to nearly swoon every time I walked past this shrine, which was opposite the bus station. It was only afterwards they told me they had been joking and it was really the entrance to Pilkington's Glassworks. Of course the friends who teased me weren't around years later when I did a well-paid personal appearance in that very building.

I was always in charge of our Maisie as she followed me through school. At the end of every day I would drag her home as fast as I could because I never wanted to miss a minute of *Mrs Dale's Diary* on the radio. It was my favourite programme, the first soap opera that I can remember. I listened to it for years.

Maisie would come out early from infant school and would be waiting for me at the senior school gates at 4.00 p.m. She was usually playing on a pile of coke, as I recall. I would grab her and run home in time to switch on *Mrs Dale*, which began at 4.15. I would sit Maisie on the settee and quickly get a crust of bread and lather butter and jam on it to keep Maisie quiet until 4.30. She was banned from speaking while *Mrs Dale* was on. I used to like *Dick Barton* as well, but *Mrs Dale's Diary* to me was like an escape. I used to try to imagine what they were all like.

The opposite sex never played much of a part in my life until I was fourteen when a boy from school kept arriving on our doorstep, and somehow we were 'going out'. He had lovely blond hair in a Tony Curtis hairdo with long sideboards. He was older than me and he was a Teddy Boy with one of those really long jackets, drainpipe trousers and crepe-soled shoes.

He had chains hanging off his jacket and he did look a bit different. He had a great big ring on one finger and we had read all about the dreaded 'chain gangs' even though we didn't quite know what they were. He was a very sweet young lad underneath, but my father peered at him over his paper and he simply could not believe what he was looking at.

It was right at the start of the Teddy Boy era. This was at the end of rationing, and I don't think anything has been as sensational as Teddy Boys. My dad could not believe it. I liked him a lot and we went out for a couple of years. I loved to go dancing at the church hall and to the occasional dance at the school.

I was tall for my age and still flat-chested. My mother used to buy me these V-necked sweaters and I used to have to wear them back to front with a big pin in the back. Later I used to pinch lovely blouses from my mother and always warn Maisie not to tell my mother, but then my mother would go to wear this blouse weeks later and it would be all scrunched up with a big hole in it. She would say, 'You've had my blouse, I know you've had it on.' I would say, 'No I haven't.'

I was not at all like all the wonderful women I had seen in the movies. They all seemed to be petite, or dark like Jane Russell, with legs like Betty Grable. To make myself a little more ample up front I used to buy specially shaped sponges to go under my dress. You could have small, medium or large depending on how voluptuous you wanted to look. But if you overdid it and got them too big they were inclined to move when you danced, which could be a bit alarming for your partner.

I once went out with another lad on a date when I had some sponges in and we were having a bit of a cuddle at the bus stop. All of a sudden his eyes sort of glazed over and he started trembling. I thought he was having a fit or something. Then I looked down to see he was gently fondling my sponges.

I couldn't feel a thing of course but he was getting

very carried away. I thought, 'Oh my God! What do I do?' I didn't know what to do so I just said, 'Oh, Oh, Oh,' a few times and then I calmed him down a bit.

I believed I died when I slept. My mother used to say that fire engines could come through the house and not wake me up. I really believed I used to die. The worst fright I had was one night when Maisie insisted she had seen a man in our room. She'd been dreaming. She wasn't that bothered but I just about screamed the house down. 'A man,' I yelled. 'Our Maisie's seen a man and he is coming to get us.' My mother came rushing in to calm me down. I think I frightened Maisie a lot more than the nightmare did. In the end my mother got into bed and slept with us that night to calm me down. I was about sixteen then.

When I left school there wasn't a great choice of jobs. If you were clever you went into an office but if you were like me you went to be a shop assistant, or into tailoring or other factory work.

But in those days men had men's jobs and women had women's jobs. You didn't see men working in cafés. You never saw a man clearing tables. You never saw girls of sixteen working in a fish and chip shop. They were always run by married couples, and old married couples at that. In those days everybody had a trade.

There was such a thing as having pride and being honourable. When I was growing up it was considered disgraceful for two lads to set about another lad. They would have been laughed at and called cowards. I don't remember ever hearing of anyone getting broken into. Everybody left their key outside the front door under a brick. If you found money or jewellery in the street you automatically handed it in to the police.

The police in those days were looked up to. After your mother and your father the next person you respected the most was a policeman.

When I first left school my mum said, 'You can come and work with me, I'll get you a job.' She was now working at a large tailoring factory on York Road, so I went there. She bought me a pinny and put these shears in my hand and said, 'You start at eight o'clock in the morning.'

When I walked in my heart sank. I thought, 'Oh my God!' They used to have *Music While You Work* blaring out from the radio at full blast. That competed with the row from the machines, and the noise was terrible. They put me on trousers and even though I had somebody to show me what to do I knew straight away that it wasn't for me. I hated it and I couldn't understand how my mother could stick it. But she just loved the feeling of friendship between the women.

With my first week's wages I wanted to get my mum and dad something really special so I stopped at the market on the way home and spent the lot on a great big pot horse. It was a huge ornament. My mum's mouth dropped open when she saw it and she said, 'I don't believe it!' But I meant well.

Yet, try as I might, I just never felt part of it. I did

try to get on and make a go of my first job but after about a month this bloke in charge came over and said gently, 'I don't think you are really cut out for this job.'

I said, 'I'm not. I hate it.' Only I didn't say it very loud because I was still very shy at that stage, if you can believe that. I talked it over with my mother. She kept saying, 'You need a trade,' and I kept saying, 'I can't stand it any more, mother.' In the end we decided I would change and become a shop assistant, so after just six weeks at the factory I moved across the road to a parade of shops just opposite where I got a job in a shoe shop called Addleman's.

I quite liked selling at first. There was none of the grinding monotony or the noise of the factory, and I liked chatting to people who came in. But the boss had a problem with a load of ghastly green suede shoes he had bought. There were boxes and boxes of them and he was desperate to get rid of them. He told me I was in for a two shilling bonus on each pair I sold.

I did quite well and managed to shift a few pairs, then this woman came in with her daughter. She was only fifteen, this girl, but she took size eight shoes and she was enormous. She must have been 18 stone, poor lass. I could tell her mother didn't have much money to spend.

I said brightly, 'What about these?' and brought out the green suede shoes. At first she didn't like them, but I kept harping on about how stylish they were and what good value. The kid was getting quite upset as I

rattled along and talked her mother gradually into buying them. The mother was convinced by then and she
was really pushing them on her daughter, who might
have been fat but she could recognise a grotty pair of
shoes when she saw them.

I looked at the girl's face and saw how miserable
she looked. Then I realised I couldn't do it. The shoes
were awful and totally wrong for this poor girl, so I
started to tell them the truth. I had quite a hard job persuading the mother that she was not missing the bargain
of the century. Finally I managed to talk her out of them.

The relief on that kid's face when she saw she
didn't have to wear those horrible shoes was almost
worth the sack that I got when the manager raced out in a
rage. He had been listening to every word and had heard
me talk my way into and then out of a certain sale. He
was definitely not impressed.

So I'd had two disastrous jobs in about four
months. At this rate I would soon be running out of
places to work. From there I went to Woolworth's
where I was put on the light bulb counter. I liked it there
but sadly I can't say I was a great success. Deep sympa-
thy with hard-up customers, I learned for the second
time, is not a great advantage to a long career in the retail
trade.

I used to feel sorry for these old age pensioners
buying a bulb with a few pennies they had scraped
together and I used to slip an extra bulb into the bag as a
bonus. The trouble was that they were all so scrupu-
lously honest that they would come back to the counter

to point out my generous mistake – usually at the top of their voices. I was soon job-hunting again. But that wasn't the soul-destroying business it is today. Then it seemed there were plenty of jobs. You could walk out of one you didn't like on a Friday and into a different one on the next Monday. I know, I frequently did just that.

I was a cinema usherette for a while, at The Star, down York Road. That was interesting. I couldn't believe the uniforms we had to wear, it was like being in a brass band, I had these big padded shoulders and tassels all over the place. I was only thin, it was a job to walk with this get-up on, and I never knew where to point my torch. I would walk round shining it at the ceiling. The audience used to say it was like a searchlight trying to pick out enemy bombers and make aeroplane noises to get me to shine it down.

They had me up in the balcony and everyone was kissing and cuddling on the back row and then up I would walk with this blasted torch. I was really popular with that. I liked watching the films but I wasn't very interested in showing people to their seats, which is a bit of a drawback for an usherette.

After I left Woolworth's my dad tried to get me on the straight and narrow. He used to go fishing with a bloke that owned a gardening shop, so I got a job there handling bulbs of a different kind. I didn't fancy it at first but my mum got the cards out and started looking into the future. 'Oh, I see this new job for you coming up in a shop.' She had a knack of getting the cards to predict exactly what she wanted to happen. She said she could see flowers and it looked a really good job for me.

So I got this job at Steven's and Rhodes's. I didn't like it but I did it because my mum had foreseen it for me. I seemed to spend most of my time in a little room at the back where I used to weigh seeds out and make tea and so on. One day this old tramp came in, at least I thought he was an old tramp, but it turned out he was a very famous painter. He wanted to paint my portrait. I just thought he was a bit odd.

Sadly I was no more successful at the garden shop. I didn't know a thing about gardening or show any signs of being likely to learn, and after a few unhappy weeks I drifted back into tailoring in a small factory that was a real slog to work in with a terrible taskmaster who made Mike Baldwin seem easy-going.

4
Married, Single, and Married Again

My parents did their level best to make sure that the early part of my life was like a long, happy, romantic film. But when I was eighteen I got a shock when I found out that in real life not everyone finds the man of their dreams and gets to live happily ever after.

Looking back, it seems incredible that I got engaged to my first husband after we'd only really known each other for about six weeks. I was young and naive and looking for someone to love. My parents liked him, so I thought it must be all right. I was soon to learn that there is a lot more to marriage than that. But we did it in style. I was the very first bride to get married at the new church, St Gregory's, opposite our house.

We had to get special permission from the bishop and it was a big thing for me as a Catholic to marry a non-Catholic because we had to promise to bring the children up within the faith. And I had six bridesmaids and a page boy. My name is still first in that register and we got in all the papers. We were married on Boxing Day, 1957.

At the very last minute as I was leaving home to get

married I suddenly decided I wanted to back out. My dad, who was going to give me away, was just turning to lock the door when I said, 'I've changed my mind, I don't want to get married.'

He thought it was just nerves, so he shoved me through the gate and said, 'Come on, you'll be all right.' I had a car to take me to the church even though it was only just down the street because I did want to arrive in style. So I swallowed my objections and went along with it. My dad seemed to be right at the time that it was much too late to change my mind. And I did have a lovely white dress.

But I wasn't all right. We just weren't good for each other. Pretty early on I realised it was not going to work out. We moved in with his grandmother and it was very difficult for all of us living in the same house. I was much, much too young and inexperienced to get married.

The basic problem was that we didn't really know each other, but by the time I realised that for sure I had made an awful mistake I was pregnant with my first child, Graham. It wasn't anybody's fault but we were always terribly hard up, and my mother used to help us out with groceries.

I knew in my heart that the marriage was over, and I went back to my mum and dad even before Graham was born. Of course they took me in and welcomed me with open arms, whatever misgivings they might have had privately. I always knew that whatever happened I could go home, and they were fantastic to me. I don't think it was a big shock to them, but it was still upsetting all the same.

Isn't it strange how you crave for something when you're pregnant? I used to eat flour. I couldn't stop. I would go into the cupboard and cram it into my mouth. It had to be self-raising. My mother used to say, 'She won't have a baby, she'll have two loaves and a bread-cake.' Mind you, Graham was a great big fat baby when he arrived: he was 9 lb 4 oz. He came into the world on 30 December 1958, in St James's Hospital. He was a lovely baby.

We tried again to make our marriage work. A friend of my mother's rented us part of her house. So, for the sake of baby Graham I suppose, we set up home again and I tried living in Hunslet, away to the south of the city. But it just didn't work out. It was a very unhappy time for me. I was still only a kid really and I just wanted to come home to my mother's all the time. Every day I used to put Graham in this big Silver Cross pram and catch two buses and a tram. It was an awful journey but it was worth it to get out of that area and back home for the day.

After that we set out to buy a house at Whitkirk, but we just couldn't keep up the mortgage. We never seemed to have enough money. When Graham was about a year old I went home for good. I knew that there was just nothing between my husband and me any more.

So there I was, at twenty, stuck with no job and a

baby to look after. They call them one-parent families nowadays, and it doesn't seem that unusual. Well, in my day I was a mother with no husband to help her, and it seemed like the end of the world. It really knocked my confidence. For a time I didn't realise what was happening to me.

In those days you had to go down to Leeds Town Hall to try to get your maintenance money, and I thought I'd die of shame. You had to have a special card. I remember my number was 997; it will always be imprinted on my brain. I used to have to go on a Monday and queue round the corner and wait for this really miserable looking man to look in a big ledger. You gave him your number and prayed that there would be some money there for you. Sometimes there was and sometimes there wasn't. It was dreadful. I was on nerve tablets for ages.

I'd had all these romantic Hollywood dreams about what I was going to do with my life. I wasn't that sure what I wanted to do but I knew I could sing – people were always asking me. But I was so depressed, I thought I had made such a mess of everything.

I used to put on a brave front and laugh and clown around like I do today, but underneath I was really very unhappy. It took me an awful long time to get myself together again, and that was when I realised how wonderful my parents really were. They just cared for me and were always there for me, which was just what I needed.

I tried to do my bit around the house, but sadly I've never been the world's most practical person. The most disastrous thing I ever did was when I decided to do some painting. With everyone out at work I had a lot of time on my hands for a change. I cleared all the food out of the pantry and painted that from top to bottom. That looked pretty good so I carried on upstairs to the toilet. I painted everything, even the cistern and the pipe coming down, and even the toilet seat. When my dad came home he went up to the loo, and unfortunately the paint was still tacky. He yelled loud enough to fetch the house down. You could see the hairs from the back of his leg stuck on the toilet seat. It must have been terribly painful for him. I steered well clear of painting for a while after that disastrous bit of do-it-yourself.

I did get a job again. I always wanted to support myself. And again I got a job at The Utilus, the tailoring factory where my mother had moved to. It was a real sweat shop. But I stuck it because there was a nursery at Quarry Hill flats nearby. In the morning I used to get off the bus, run into the nursery and leave Graham, run out of the other side and into the factory. I used to get reduced rates at the nursery because I was separated. It used to cost me six shillings a week, while the full price for the other mothers was £3. This horrible woman who used to run it used to call out in a really loud voice, 'Just the six shillings from you,' to rub it in with everyone else that I was getting something on the cheap. I used to think, 'I'll kill that woman.' I used to look at her and every time I used to silently plead with her, 'Please don't say that again.'

She used to love to humiliate me. But my mother used to insist I got everything I was entitled to. She used to say, 'Look, me and your dad have worked all our lives and paid all our tax. You're not getting anything free, because we've paid in.'

But I hated having to throw myself on the mercy of the authorities. People who have never been hard up just can't imagine the feelings that poor people are put through.

There was another place where you could go for free shoes. My mother was kind and she was generous but she used to say, 'Look, if there is anything you can get, get it. You deserve it.' So one time I got this form entitling me to get some shoes for Graham. It was horrible. There were all black shoes, all different sizes but all the same awful style. As I tried them on his little feet I thought, I will never ever come here again, ever. And I never did. And he never wore those shoes, they were so blinking dreadful.

Maisie was good to me as well, even though she was much younger. And it wasn't all pain and agony. I did have a laugh or two. I remember taking Maisie to the horror film *Dracula* at the Majestic. Before we went I warned her firmly, 'If you're frightened and you do anything to show me up, I'll never take you anywhere again.' But when we got there it was me that was scared. I finished up sitting with my handbag in front of my face, whimpering. I was hopeless. Someone would only have to rustle a paper bag and I would think there was someone after me. Maisie told me afterwards how embarrassed she was. I was twenty-one and terrified of horror films. To be honest, I think I still am.

We went a lot to the cinemas around us. There were so many in those days – the Star, the Shaftesbury and the Hillcrest. We used to get the family allowance on a Tuesday, so we used to go on the Wednesday to the pictures.

Gradually I started going out again a little. I couldn't go out that often but my mother would babysit one or maybe two nights a week.

After a time I went out on Tuesdays and Fridays. I met an electrician called Don one night in a pub in Leeds called the Fforde Green near Roundhay Park. I know it's an old joke, but I think I was his first shock. It was packed out. It certainly was nothing like love at first sight, but I know I did get a funny feeling and somehow I knew we were going to get together. I can't explain how, but I knew it was sort of inevitable. It was just as though someone had pointed at us both and said, 'That's it.'

He was sitting there talking with some friends of mine from school. He looked all right, but nothing special. He was just very quiet and serious looking. They say the quiet ones are the worst, don't they? I didn't know then that he had been working away in Oldham and hadn't slept for two nights.

I was really talking to some other friends and Don

happened to be sitting next to me. I was mucking about a bit and tapping him on the shoulder and asking silly questions. I was just larking around because I was out and free from responsibility for once.

But one of the blokes with him had been out with one of my friends before, and that couple wanted to go for a Chinese meal after the pub closed. Don and I found ourselves tagging along to make up the numbers. He attacked his food as though he hadn't eaten for a week. I only ate half of mine and he finished it up. I remember thinking, 'My God. I wonder if he kisses like he eats.' He was really shovelling it in.

At the end of the night he said, 'I can take you home.' I said, 'No.' He said, 'I've got a car,' and being awkward I said, 'I don't like cars.' But he gave me a lift home in the end. And he asked to take me out again. I told him that I could only get out on Tuesdays and Fridays and that on Tuesdays I went to the White Horse. When I got there on Tuesday night he was sitting outside, and this friend of mine, Glenda, said, 'Ooh, there, that bloke there.' I said, 'Yes,' then as we approached the car I said, 'Oh hello,' and he just said, all cool like, 'Hi. What are you doing on Friday?' I said, 'Well, I might be coming in here,' and we went in for a drink without him.

On the Friday he was there again and Glenda said, 'Ooh, there's that funny bloke there again. There's something not right about him.' He would just keep asking me if I was going in the pub, but he would stay outside.

He said, 'I might see you again.' I said, 'Oh, might you?' all casual and cool. But he was working away and never quite knew when he would be back in Leeds. A few times afterwards I used to see him hanging around outside this pub where we'd met. I didn't realise he wanted to see me again. He didn't know where I lived because I wouldn't tell him.

This went on for about four weeks and I was getting a bit worried because he didn't ask me out but he was always hanging around. I thought he might be a bit funny. Glenda used to call him 'I might see you'.

Eventually he was there sitting in his car with his arm out, tapping the roof, and he said, 'If you're going in there I might come in tonight. I'm just going to see a friend of mine first.' We went in the pub and a bit later Don and his pal came in. I couldn't believe he had actually made it inside. That was how we started going out together. But still he never spoke. I remember about the fourth or fifth time he disappeared for a while and when he came back he was soaking wet. I asked him what had happened and he said, 'It's raining outside. You'll talk to anyone but me, so I thought I would go for a walk.' He had gone out of the pub and come back and I'd not noticed.

One of the first proper dates we had was a drive out to a really nice pub in Scarcroft, just on the edge of Leeds. This was really something for me because I never used to venture away from the bus routes. My mother gave me some advice about lads: 'Never go off a bus route. Never go away from the lights.' Every boy-friend I ever had I used to kiss under lamp-posts; it didn't matter whether there were double-decker buses passing or what. She used to say, 'Never ever go in a doorway with any lad.' It was imprinted on my brain.

It was snowing. I'll never forget, he had this mac on with his collar up and this really serious face. And he used to talk out the side of his mouth. I felt like I was Hilda Baker in some sort of crazy comedy show.

It felt really weird. It's no distance to this village but in the dark with no buses passing and with snow pelting down it felt really creepy. We got to this pub and I kept thinking, 'Oh, I don't know him really. He could be some sort of maniac. He could kill me.' When we got to the pub I was all of a dither. He got me a drink and I just sat there and had about three sips and I was so nervous I blurted out, 'I want to go home.'

He looked really shocked. I said, 'I don't like being so far away from the places I know.' He said, 'I'm not going to rape you!' I said, 'No, you're not. But you can take me home.'

We got back in the car and I realised I had left my old umbrella in the pub. Don went back for it for me and I thought that was kind but I didn't really want the umbrella because it was really past it. He put it up and there were just four spokes sticking up. That was our first date. After that it was 'I might see you again next week' for quite a while.

Don was the oldest of eight, and he had six sisters.

Me and my guitar. Unfortunately I never did learn to play it.

Top left: My first wedding. The marriage was fine. Living together wasn't quite so easy.

Top right: On holiday in Blackpool with my friend Joan when I was 20.

Above right: I was a blushing bridesmaid when I was eight years old for my Auntie Nellie and Uncle Alex.

Above: I loved to enter talent contexts on holiday. Here I was singing away at Cayton Bay, Scarborough.

Top left: Don and me out on the town at the Mecca in Leeds.

Top right: I spent my last half-a-crown to sit on Dennis Tanner's knee.

Above left: First prize in Miss Harp Larger. Fame didn't go to my head.

Above right: I won a talent context at Cayton Bay.

Top left: My Dad and my Mum.

Top right: Pregnant again!

Above: Our family back in 1969. That's Graham at the back and the girls from the left are baby Julie, Dawn and Ann.

That's the photo from the Duckworth's front room. It's supposed to be Vera and Terry but it's really me and Julie.

Top left: Lynne Perrie and me leading the pickets in the BBC's *Leeds United* back in 1973.

Top right: With Lynne again, this time in my very first *Coronation Street* scene. Vera's arrival.

Above: Bedelia Conroy, landlady of the Feathers Hotel, was a smashing part in *Crown Court* that gave me a real boost.

Top: Well someone had to start the work on our new Coronation Street Studios Tours.

Above: Dustin Gee did such affectionate impressions of Vera that I couldn't help but laugh.

Trust me to hit the headline at the Royal Variety Show when my dress got tucked into my knickers by the man fixing my microphone!

He was used to looking after them all and being left in charge, so he never stood any nonsense. He wouldn't let a woman get the better of him. So I imagine he thought it was no problem to sort out this woman who was on tranquillisers.

Then Don got work at St Theresa's School and I used to see him when I went down to the shops with Graham, and I was looking after my niece as well at the time. Don used to come over and chat with us, but we were never love's young dream. I used to think, 'I'll never be able to get on with this bloke.'

For a long time I didn't feel totally relaxed with him. It's hard to explain, but I never felt I could say 'Knickers' in his presence. If you can say 'Knickers' to someone it means that you have crossed the barrier, that you get on well with them.

Graham was about two then, and Don was very good with him. But things never ran that smoothly. He offered to take me and Graham to Scarborough for the day and I got all ready and then he didn't turn up on time. He was about half an hour late. By the time he came I was fuming. He was supposed to be round at nine o'clock but he slept in and I'd been really looking forward to getting out for the day and I sort of flipped. I got my best things off and started cleaning the fire out for something to do. When he did arrive I went berserk at him and a lot of my sadness and frustration came out. It was the first time he had seen my temper – but certainly not the last, I have to say.

I felt really disappointed, let down and angry, so I let him have it. After a while I calmed down and we did go and had a really nice day out.

I didn't have a lot of different clothes, and usually when I went out I would wear the same little black dress. I often think now, when I look at my overflowing wardrobes, of the times when I wore that little black dress.

I've always had the ability to bounce back from things. Life can be hard, and Don and I always argued. But we laughed a lot as well. He used to love winding me up a bit and then making up afterwards.

I had never been to London until Don decided to take me. We went with a workmate of his and his girlfriend. We went to the Ideal Home Exhibition and stayed for a night in one of those small hotels near King's Cross. Don had worked down there before and he wanted to show me round a bit. He had been in this pub called The Rising Sun in Bethnal Green. It was so crowded nobody could sit down and they wouldn't drink the draught beer because it was so bad down south. They just drank bottled beer and then dropped the bottles on the floor. It was a bit rough, you might say.

In those days the gap between north and south seemed much larger. The motorways hadn't been finished then and it took hours to drive down. I think they thought Northerners were a bit thick because of our accents, but that never bothered me. I liked the life down there, and I enjoyed the weekend. It opened my eyes to the fact there was life outside Leeds. This was the height of the popularity of Carnaby Street. We went there and to Petticoat Lane on the Sunday morning.

Another Saturday night we went off to Blackpool on a bus trip to see the illuminations, but the traffic was horrendous. We left Leeds abut six o'clock at night, and didn't get to Blackpool until about eleven. We had about an hour there and then the bus set off back again.

We went out for a couple of years and gradually got closer and closer. He used to come to our house just about every night. My dad used to say darkly, 'Familiarity breeds contempt.' I think it was my dad's way of saying, 'Can't you have a rest from him?' Even when Don was working away he used to come. I was still very bruised from my first marriage and not at all in a hurry to get married again. In any case it took a lot longer for your divorce to come through in those days and I was still married.

Graham always thought my dad was his dad. As he grew up I tried to explain that he was really his grandad because his mates used to say, 'Isn't your dad old?' And then little Graham would pipe up, 'He's not my dad. He's my grandad.'

When I started going out with Don seriously I said to Graham, 'Can't you call Don Dad?' And he would say, 'No. This is not his house. This is my grandad's house.' But when we got a flat together he started calling Don Dad straight away.

Of course I got pregnant again soon afterwards. Don just said to his mother one night, 'I'm leaving,' and he arrived with his bed and his Army blanket. They were warm, those Army blankets, but it was hardly enough to set up home with. We had bought a double bed for ourselves, but we needed a bed for Graham.

It was when we went on holiday to Wallace's Holiday Camp at Cayton Bay near Scarborough that suddenly everything happened to me. I won a heater. I won a singing contest. I came second in Miss Harp Lager. And when we came home we got the key to a flat in Southwood Tors. It was fantastic. Everything just all seemed to happen at once. It wasn't a very big flat, and it meant I had to lug the pram up three flights of stairs every time I went out, but it was still our place.

Then when I came back from holiday I found I had won a sweep at the church which was a prize of £25, so we went to Bridlington for another holiday. I've always believed in enjoying my life as I go along. But up until then I hadn't had that much to celebrate.

Don and I had loads of happy times. At last I had a man who would really look after me. Don has always had a forceful personality and so have I. That has meant we have had an 'interesting' relationship. We have never been one of those gooey-eyed, lovey-dovey couples who spend hours gazing into each other's eyes. But particularly in those early days I was very happy to lean on his broad shoulders.

Coronation Street was always part of our lives. When I was about seven months pregnant with Anne we were on holiday at Wallace's Holiday Camp. They used to get someone from *Coronation Street* to make an appearance, and Dennis Tanner was there – or Philip Lowrie the actor, I should say.

I'll never forget. It was half a crown to have your photograph taken with him. I queued up for ages to sit on his knee in 1966 at Cayton Sands. I spent my insurance money to pay for that treat. I didn't mind, I think it was worth it to sit on his knee. I really liked him in *Coronation Street*. He was really nice and it was unbelievable to meet him and actually sit on his knee.

I can even remember my sister-in-law having a baby at home and the doctor was there and all the kids wanted to watch *Coronation Street* while upstairs she was lying on the bed with her legs in the air. The doctor and I were laughing to think about them watching *Coronation Street* rather than our very real drama.

I got a job at Littlewood's in the staff canteen. The priest at St Gregory's helped us to get Graham into school early so I could work. But it was a horrible place to work. This buzzer used to go and I would be standing there in my little white overall and my little white hat and thinking, 'Right, I'm all ready.' There would be trays of cups of tea and coffee all there waiting.

But then the staff would arrive and it was just pandemonium. One would want a coffee with sugar and no milk, and somebody else wanted tea with plenty of sugar, and I couldn't take it in quickly enough. It was a nightmare. My nerves were shot at that time and I simply couldn't stand the job. I said to the boss that I would rather sweep floors. So I left there.

In those days if you were pregnant you got married.
I loved Don but we always battled. It was hard for both
of us at the start. He had been used to his mother getting
up at 6.30 in the morning to send him off to work with a
cooked breakfast. I wasn't much of a cook and I certainly wasn't used to rushing round to fetch and carry for
a man. Attitudes were different in those days. It was
expected of a woman. All of a sudden Don found himself going from really good home-cooked food to eating
everything out of a tin. The first time I washed Don's
lovely sweaters that his mum had knitted him they all
shrank.

We never seemed to have much spare money even
though Don had a good job. He sold his car, a Ford Con-
sul, for £300 before we got married to buy furniture and
carpets. £300 was a lot of money then, and we managed.
By the time we got married we even got another car, a
little Austin A30.

I remember going in the supermarket and getting a
basket and buying six knives, six forks, two dusters,
four cups and four saucers. We weren't planning on
doing a lot of entertaining. The night before the official
flit everything was behind my mother's door. There was
a really bad thunderstorm, with lightning flashing and
thunder booming out. I was awake all night wondering
if I should go down and cover all my bits and pieces.

Once I went out and bought a second-hand washing machine, because I was washing by hand or going to
my mother's to do it, and the shop was going to deliver

it. But when I told Don he went mad. He said we couldn't afford one. He had budgeted how much we had to spend and knew we could not afford that washer. I hadn't done much work with all my problems and looking after Graham, and he knew cash was tight. Believe me, those early days were hard, and he had no money to spare. But he was very good with Graham. He used to say, 'I will bring him up as if he was my natural son.' And he did.

Our marriage was hardly the occasion romantic dreams are made of. We had already been living together for six months and we just got on the bus with my mother and father and his mother and father and went down to the Registry Office. It was 21 January 1965.

There are no photographs because I couldn't bear the idea of being pictured as a bride seven months on. I remember the men talked about fishing all the way there. My father and his father were the witnesses at our wedding and all they could think of to talk about was flaming fishing.

Afterwards we had our 'reception' in Lewis's restaurant on the top floor, just the six of us. There was a pantomime on in Leeds at the time and the waitress looked at us all dressed up and asked, 'Are you going to the pantomime?'

'No,' I said. 'We've just been.'

We couldn't afford to do anything more and we didn't really want to make a fuss. We wanted to have a quiet wedding because we had told lots of people who lived near us that we were already married. Living 'in sin' was really frowned upon in those days. Today no one bats an eyelid. We were married on a Wednesday and I was back at work the next day.

I had never been in a Registry Office before and I have never been in one since. It was so cold and impersonal. We just couldn't afford anything. I got married wearing a borrowed fur coat. It was one of the worst days of my life. I still try to block it out of my mind. I didn't like any part of that day. That is why we never send anniversary cards. Who wants to remember that? It was just awful. We only got one present – a paper rack from one of Don's sisters.

Our first daughter, Dawn Elizabeth, was born on 19 March, so straight away we had two children to feed and clothe and care for. She got her name because she was born at dawn. The feeling of responsibility was a real shock, for both of us I think. But she was a really good baby.

To earn us extra money Don used to collect the money for Provident club cheques. Everyone lived on that sort of credit in those days. But it turned out that the first people he had to visit were next door! They were a terrible long way behind with their payments with no sign of ever being able to catch up.

I said, 'Pack this job up, it's too embarrassing.' He stuck it for a while but it wasn't a happy time.

I think the final straw came when he sent me to pick

up the Provident turkey for our Christmas dinner. One of the few perks of the job was that the firm provided you with a free turkey. Don gave me this form and I went off, with two young kids in tow as usual, to collect our big treat.

When I got to the butcher's my heart sank. There was a massive queue stretching way down the road and round the corner. But I didn't have a choice. It was freezing cold, the kids were miserable, but a free turkey was a free turkey and I wasn't going to miss out on that.

When I finally reached the counter I proudly handed over my piece of paper and looked down to choose a really succulent-looking bird. The butcher looked at the paper and said, 'What's this?'

I said, 'This is paid for. It's for my Provident turkey.' There was deep consultation behind the counter, and gradually any feeling of jollity and seasonal spirit I'd been feeling drained out of me. The queue had been stopped by my interruption and suddenly people on both sides of the counter waited until judgement was pronounced on my plea for a free bird.

'We don't deal with Provident,' said the big red-faced head butcher with an air of unarguable finality. I was in the wrong shop. Somehow I turned on my heel and marched the kids out without bursting into tears, but I'm not sure how. I trudged sadly off to find the right butcher's shop and begin the whole miserable queueing process all over again.

Money was always tight, but that didn't stop us

enjoying life. Some of the best times we had were at the weekend when we used to get up early to pack a load of sandwiches and then set off for a day in Scarborough. We would just play with the kids on the beach and walk round Peasholme Park, but the sun always seemed to be shining. We might not have been able to afford to go into cafés for a proper meal, but we managed.

My daughter Anne's favourite habit was wandering off on the beach. You'd look round and she would be gone and suddenly we would be arranging search parties. I guess she took after me for mischief.

5
On the Club Circuit

About this time Don came up with the brainwave that changed my life. In our little flat we used to have a mural, or a Muriel as Hilda Ogden used to call her wall painting. In fact it was rather like Hilda's mountain scene, and I could just imagine Don gazing into it and thinking up his plot to increase our income.

I had always sung a lot and I suppose I can't have had a bad voice as people used to keep asking me to get up. But I was never that sure of myself, I was often short of confidence, so Don took the initiative for me. He put me down for an audition as a singer. I'd only sung in pubs or at family get-togethers really, but Don just said, 'I've heard you sing and you are good.'

I had sung at holiday camps and even won talent contests. I won first prize one night. It was £10, presented to me by the actor Jack Watling, which was an awful lot in those days and we really needed the money as usual. But it was a charity night at this holiday camp and there was fund-raising going on for handicapped kids.

I was so moved by those kids that I handed my prize money straight back. Don was very good about it because we hadn't even got the petrol money to get home. We were absolutely skint. Don had to borrow from his brother Jack to get us home. But those kids were desperate.

But I was still on tranquillisers and I'd just given birth to my second child, so it was a shock to me when Don came back just six weeks after Dawn was born and told me he'd put my name down at Jim Windsor's Club.

He had given me a new name as well. He decided that Sylvia Butterfield was a bit of a mouthful for show business so he had decided I should become Elizabeth Dawn – reversing the names we had just given our baby daughter.

Why he called me Elizabeth I'll never know. It felt far too posh for me. I did once have another stage name – for a while I had called myself Lisa Barry. I thought if I changed my name I might do better. Then I had a phase of wanting to be called Esther Franklyn.

He never said anything at the time but it was when I won the talent contest at Cayton Bay that Don got the idea to put me in for a proper audition. There were professional singers in that contest and I beat them. But I only knew a couple of songs and I was soon running out of repertoire. And there is a world of difference between standing up in a talent contest when you're on holiday with no pressure on you and facing up to entertain an audience in a club run by a hard-nosed concert secretary.

I did well enough at the audition to land three bookings straight away. I was amazed! I'd gone into that audition a bag of nerves and came out a professional singer.

But I soon found out that it wasn't always going to be as easy as that.

At the audition I sang 'More'. You know, 'More than the greatest love the world has known'. It's still one of my favourite songs. This was in the days before the agents took over and it was the concert secretaries who came to see what new talent was on the market. It was pretty frightening, literally singing for your supper. The pay was £3.50 a night for my first night.

The first two bookings went all right. I just handed over the music of the handful of songs I knew to the musicians and got on with it. I was nervous, of course, even though I knew I had a good voice. But I didn't realise that the musicians were transposing the music into the right key for me.

My third job was at a club in Halifax, and the organist there was not up to transposing the music for me. He cheerfully played every song in the wrong key, and I sounded dreadful. I learned a lot that night. It was all new to us and we asked around and found a young lad in Leeds called Mike Terry who could transpose all the music into the right key for me. Mike had a music shop but he was an act as well so he knew what my problems were. I used to go every Saturday for a while and he used to sit looking at me rather strangely. I found out after a week or two that he was a female impersonator. He did a very good Winifred Attwell!

Work in clubs was never easy. But it's a great learning ground. Club audiences must be the most demanding audiences in the world. They have come to meet their friends, have a drink and a game of bingo and if the 'turn' wants to distract them from that then it has to be good. They challenge you to make them listen.

You have no rehearsal. You just pull up with your gear and it's 'on stage'. I learned quickly that you just have to keep smiling whatever happens. You see, when you sing in the clubs you are a professional and if you are getting paid they expect something special before they will readily part with their hard-earned brass. Don says now that I went down very well lots of times and I can't have been that bad to get asked back. But my memories of those days are mainly of battling against awful nerves.

When I first started I used to collect all the family pictures and stand them up somewhere in whatever passed for a dressing room. I would look at the snaps of the kids and my mother's picture and I used to say, 'Oh God, please let me be good tonight, don't let me suffer.'

Then I would go out and do my best. It seems incredible now but when we first started we did five singing spots in an evening. So you could go down really well three times and then die in the last two because the audience were half plastered. And the pay was £3 or £4.

Don was a real prop to me in those early days together. I felt so guilty and unhappy about having a broken marriage behind me. That was when I needed strong people round me. When I went back home my mother was very strong and supportive. She got me through the worst. Then Don came along and he was reliable. He was the man of the house and his chair was his chair, just like it had been with my dad. Sometimes I feel I should have broken out and become more independent and made my life alone. Deep down inside I wanted to be free of everything.

I went again to have my fortune told when Dawn was a baby and I was pregnant with Anne. It was at Bridlington, where there was yet another gypsy looking into the future. I have always been fascinated by predictions – I think I've crossed that many palms with silver I must have bought my own caravan by now.

When I went into her caravan I was struck by her presence straight away. She had a real look of the mystical about her. She began by doing my cards and she said, 'That little girl with you is very artistic and she will draw the clothes she will wear.' Then she said I would have another girl, which I duly did, and went on to say to me, 'You will do very well in life and you will have a house with a drive that will have space for several cars to park.'

I liked that a lot, and happily it has come true. But she also said, 'You will not live to a big age.' I didn't like that bit so much, and in quiet moments I often wonder. Now I do have a house with a drive that will hold a few cars, and Dawn is very artistic. But my mother died at 57 and I'm 53 now, so in my sombre moments I wonder if I will go early as well.

We very quickly had two more daughters, so looking after them was just about a full-time job in itself. It meant I could only really do the clubs at the weekend. I suffered terribly with my nerves. They would start on a Wednesday and build up through Thursday and Friday until I went on at the weekend almost with the shakes. I laugh when I think of that – and I used to laugh then, to hide my feelings. That was my mother coming out in me, I suppose. Always put on a brave front.

Don was working then and earning a reasonable wage as an electrician, but me singing in the clubs meant the difference between living reasonably well and having some luxuries. You could earn what was a week's wage for an ordinary family in one night in the clubs. When I first started it was about £6.

Singing in the clubs certainly gave me an apprenticeship in show business. I learned that a little bit of cheek can often take you a long way.

Once I had my picture taken holding a guitar. We used to get hand-out photographs to try to drum up our reputations. One of the chaps who did mine was a guitarist in one of the groups. As he had his guitar with him, for a joke I stood holding it for the picture, flashing my legs in a mini-skirt. Just to give it a bit of life.

But the trouble was that when they picked up this picture at one of the clubs they thought they were getting an instrumental/vocalist. That was a laugh! I couldn't play a note on the guitar. I had to turn up with a bandage on my finger to give me an excuse for not playing it. When I got there the bumptious little concert secretary was astonished. 'Do you mean you're not going to play? The club is full.' He was very unimpressed.

That was bad enough, but one night we even turned up at the wrong club! We had two bookings that weekend. One night we were in Doncaster and the next night we were in Hull. But somehow we managed to get the dates mixed up. We travelled all the way over to Hull to this club and we were just putting our gear up when another act arrived. The club secretary was full of smiles as he told us, 'You're here tomorrow night, not tonight.'

Don rushed off and rang the club in Doncaster to explain what had happened. We humped all the gear back into the car and drove all the way back. It took ages to get back because this was in the days before motorways. We did manage to be there in time to go on, but they still docked my money. I got £10 instead of £20.

After Dawn was born we moved from the flat to a smart new maisonette in Winmoor Way. It was lovely there; it was a new estate. Lots of young families moved in, and I really loved it. Anne was born there and so was Julie. Anne weighed 8 lb 4 oz and Julie was 9 lb 4 oz.

Having kids is never easy, and having four little ones at once is a real trial. But I loved having a big family. Life was never dull.

We tried to bring them up the way we knew, that right was right and older people deserve respect. They might not be very fashionable values these days, but my mother and father knew a thing or two about right and wrong.

I wanted them to be taught, as I had, to have manners and to know how to behave and be thoughtful with other people. I don't like the way a lot of children today have no respect for anyone.

They have all done well in their different ways. It is not easy being brought up with a mother who is in a soap opera. It means she often becomes public property just when you want to have a quiet family time.

Dawn is now at college in Liverpool studying fine art. Julie works in personnel at Granada. Graham lives in York and works in computers. And Anne is married and lives with her family in Italy.

Just after Anne was born I had an experience that really shocked me. My granny died. I know it happens to all of us but to me it was still an awful thing. I don't think I had seen a dead body before then.

Anne was six weeks old when my Auntie Nellie ran over for me. She shouted, 'Come over, I think your granny's died.' She took me into my granny's house and she was there, still sitting but lifeless. My auntie said, 'Watch her while I go and get somebody.' It sounds awful but she just didn't want her to fall. I just stood there staring. It was horrible.

I'll never forget the feelings I had. I used to love my grandmother Shaw. She lived in a block of flats near our maisonette and I used to do her shopping for her.

Death just really shocked me. I simply couldn't believe it, looking at my own grandmother, who had always seemed so vibrant and alive, sitting there dead. Every line went out of her face. Her complexion was all smooth and it was just as if she had gone back to being a young girl.

When I saw her again, before she was buried, she looked old again. But I think the thing that upset me even more was her belongings. Her flat obviously needed to be cleaned out, but I went over a couple of days after she died and everything had been cleared up and it was in a pile in the middle of the room, her clothes and everything. I know it has to be done and I knew it then, but it just seemed so sad to see my poor granny's things laid out there.

I remember picking up a shawl that I had knitted for her. I don't think I was a full shilling because I can recall sitting with this shawl and just picking up a curl of my granny's hair that must have become attached. I sat wearing this shawl, and pulling this curl of my granny's hair through my fingers. I must have been in another world. I put the hair inside a piece of black velvet and kept it in a box.

I had that box for about three years. My mother called one day and we were just chatting, the kids were playing and we were having a cup of coffee, and I told her about it. She went mad. She said, 'You've got what?' I said, 'I've got some of my granny's hair.' I got it out and showed her and she grabbed it and threw it in the fire. She said, 'Ugh! How on earth could you?'

But I still kept the shawl. And when they asked me what else I wanted from my granny's things I picked her reading glasses. Now I know that they were of no practical use to me. But they just held a memory. I used to put them on and think, 'My granny looked through these for years.'

At this time I was building on a tough apprenticeship in show business. I would always be a bundle of nerves as Don drove me to the club. Then I would give the band the music and desperately hope that the audience was going to be good.

My worst night was in a miners' welfare club at Rossington, near Doncaster. Cannon and Ball were on the bill and it was a really difficult night. There were loads of people who had come down to work in Yorkshire and they were really rough. They just didn't want to listen to me, and in the end I lost my temper up on the stage and did the unforgivable and swore at them.

They were all shouting around and not taking any notice so I said down the microphone, 'If you're not going to listen, I'll just go home.' 'Well ★★★★ off then,' they shouted and then I saw red and swore back. I know it was unprofessional, but I was just so frustrated. It was so difficult for me to get keyed up enough to get up on stage there that if I got that sort of reception it really upset me. I know you're not supposed to take it personally, but I did.

Club artists are the warmest people in the world. They work endlessly for charity, giving lots of nights free without any thought of recognition.

In a way I suppose the clubs were the start of Vera because I was not content with just singing, I used to try to inject a bit of comedy into my act. I like a joke and I found audiences loved a daft remark or two to break the ice.

It was very hard doing the clubs in those days. With four young children to look after, the last thing you feel like at the end of the day is getting yourself dolled up and going off to a night club to sing songs. But life was a battle for loads of people, and that was our way of buying ourselves a decent life. I desperately wanted my kids to have good clothes and decent holidays. Just like when my mother gritted her teeth and worked like a Trojan to operate those three presses, when it came to it I realised I had to buckle down and do my stuff in the clubs and always, always keep smiling.

Coming off stage after your act, particularly after you've gone down well and generated some applause, and going right back to changing nappies was very hard. In some ways I felt that it was doing my head in, playing these two roles of singer and housewife.

We had some right old bangers to travel around in. One night we wrote a car off. The most frightening experience came early one morning when we were driving back to Leeds from Hull. Don was at the wheel of our aged Ford Zephyr and in the days before the M62 it took hours to wend our way across country. I had flaked out in the front seat after another exhausting day and Don was fighting tiredness at the wheel.

He got us to within half a mile of home and he must have nodded off. We mounted the pavement and hit a lamp-post which snapped off and was carried along on the roof of the car. The windscreen went and we stopped about a yard from the next lamp-post. That was when I woke up with steam fizzing out of the radiator into the car – it was really frightening.

I woke up and screamed. I was desperate to get out, but my door was smashed and wouldn't open. I had no clothes on under my big brown coat. I had taken my pantie girdle off and thrown my wig into the back seat, and you could say I was hardly looking my best. I reached for my wig and rammed it on back to front. As I scrambled out of the window a woman came out of her house, took me in and gave me a cup of tea. She must have thought, 'My God! What has she been doing?' I must have looked a total wreck, and when I realised how lucky we had been I started shaking again.

Don told the police that he had swerved to avoid a cat, and I think they believed him. Nobody wants to admit dropping asleep at the wheel. It was quite an old policeman, and he was more upset than we were. He came back to our house and we ended up giving him a cup of tea! I think the fact that we were both relaxed and fast asleep saved us from serious injury. My only cut came when I scratched myself on Don's radio scrambling out through the back seat. My wig went on over my own hair, which I didn't realise was full of bits of glass from the windscreen.

The car was a write-off, of course, but it was the time of the petrol crisis and we were short of money as usual so Don and a pal went next day to the garage the car had been towed into and siphoned out all the petrol. We couldn't afford to leave that!

It was a terrifying experience but there was no time to get over it. I was singing the next night at a club in Aubrey in Wakefield and we had to get a taxi there.

We had some awful times with ropey cars. Once Don had bumped the car at the front and we couldn't afford to have it repaired. He never told me about it. Everywhere we went for weeks people were staring at us and I didn't realise that the headlight and wing were all smashed up.

We once broke down on the way to a club in York and I finished up pushing the car for what seemed like miles before I could go on stage to sing. I think you could say it wasn't exactly the big time.

Until you have been on stage at a working men's club in front of a Saturday night audience of 1,000 people on their big night out of the week you don't quite know what fear is. They are all dressed up with their wives by their sides, and this is it: the turn. I didn't just have butterflies in my stomach – I had giant tarantulas.

Maisie always says my life has been like Rocky Graziano's life story. I've had an enormous struggle, but I've always been going to make it because I was special. I don't know so much about that, I've certainly felt like I've taken a few punches on the way. But somebody up there has liked me.

I've never been afraid of hard work – I always wanted to earn a bit extra. And it wasn't just from singing in the clubs. I did all sorts of jobs.

I worked in a factory, screwing the tops on toothpaste tubes, and the foreman liked me and said he was going to put me on quality control. But that meant I had to take samples from each line, weigh them and get the average. It was a bit baffling and I used to have to go home at night and find out from Don how to do it. It was a plum job, but I didn't want it because it took me away from the other girls, my friends. I said, 'Put me back on the bench – I'll clean, I'll do anything.' I ended up cleaning toilets after that so I couldn't have a laugh with my mates in any case.

For a while I used to run catalogues, persuading people to buy things for the commission it earned me. Then I was an Avon lady for a while. That was fun. It was hard work but I have such happy memories of those days – I had some experiences. We were living in a maisonette. Once, when I was eight months pregnant, which got to feel like a pretty permanent state for me, Don was watching television while I went out to this big block of flats to do my 'Avon calling' routine.

Men would always invite you in, so it was better to arrive after they had got home from work. They would say, 'Come in love,' and then shout to the wife when you were halfway in, 'There's someone to see you.' You would walk in and there would be the woman laid out in her corsets, and you would know that never in a million years would she want anyone to see her looking like that. I would go, 'Hello! Avon calling!' and then say, 'Oh, sorry.'

Mind you, I sometimes got myself into funny situations like that. One night I knocked on this door and I could hear this really weird music coming from inside. This bloke opened the door and he looked very, very strange. My heart sank and I didn't know what to do. He had just a shirt on and I could see all his legs but I didn't like to look too closely. Well, the shock!

I certainly didn't wait there to see if there was a lady of the house. I just panicked and made a run for it. I bolted down ten flights of stairs and round to our house as fast as I could. I ran in and gasped to Don that I had just been scared stiff by a man with no trousers on. He grunted and said, 'Just a minute, I'm watching the film.' I was so mad that I whacked him with my bag. We've often laughed together about that night since then.

I also had a spell selling wigs, curly wigs that is, that were the spitting image of the one worn by Vera Duckworth. I never knew then that I was going to finish up wearing one for a living for 20 years. Wigs had been really pricey until then, but these nylon ones were quite a good price.

It seemed a good way to make a bit extra. This man came to our house with all his range to show me and start me off. He had a suitcase full of wigs, and the most popular was the curly one like Vera's. Anne was just six weeks old when I started. I had to go to people's houses and try to persuade them a curly wig would brighten up their lives.

I didn't always keep Don fully in the picture about my various business enterprises. More than once I was having a wig party when he arrived home early from work. I would panic and usher all the women out the back door and bung the wigs in the oven so he didn't know. I didn't want him to know exactly how much I was making. It's often handy to have some money of your own. And he didn't like anyone in the house.

He would walk in and I would sit back and try to look

alluring. 'Hello, love. Have you had a good day?' But once he opened the oven and fifteen wigs fell out, so I was found out – much to Don's delight.

I was quite good at selling. I was helped by the way I was never short of something to say. The wigs were on hire purchase, of course, and even though I had no hairdressing experience I sold a lot. For a time there were more Vera Duckworths walking round our estate than you could imagine.

Quite a few of my wig parties were at really posh houses where I think it was just entertainment for the residents. I don't think they really wanted to buy a wig, they just wanted a bit of fun. I was always half asleep on my feet because I'd been up half the night making feeds. Once I curled a top knot on twelve women's heads. I did feel incredibly weird: I never spoke to them because they were all posh and spoke properly. I was a bit like a French maid, I never opened my mouth. It went well for a while but then a lot of them stopped paying for them and they used to send a red van round to collect all the wigs that weren't paid for. I was on good commission. At the time I thought the bloke that supplied the wigs must have been making a fortune, but not many people paid him.

Then I had a spell organising lingerie parties. We used to have parties in people's houses and dress up in all this lacy underwear. It was fun to see loads of women dressed up in baby doll pyjamas, especially if they were about 15 stone. We really had a laugh. It was like the one

Vera had in the Street. I was an organiser for Pippa Dee Pantie Parties and one or two other firms, and I loved it.

On that estate we were all in the same boat, struggling to bring up young kids with not very much money, so any cheap entertainment was always welcome. I did Tupperware parties as well.

After a time we moved to a larger house in Morrit Avenue. It was a really old house, full of oak beams, and I loved it. Mind you, I wasn't quite so sure about it after I found out it was haunted. One night my daughter had a friend to sleep the night and she woke up and said that she had seen a man bending over Dawn.

I said, 'Don't be so silly. There are no ghosts here.' I laughed and said, 'If you get a visit from a man in the middle of the night, send him down to me.'

But one of my other daughters also reckoned she had seen something, so I wasn't quite so sure. Then a couple of months later I had a frightening nocturnal experience of my own. I always left the landing light on for the children. I was lying dozing, being gradually lulled to sleep by the sound of Don snoring, when I saw something move in this shaft of light that came into the room from the landing.

As I lay there transfixed with fear the figure of a man came into our room. His face was deathly white. He was carrying a bag and he had a jacket on with a zip up the front like the sort of jacket Bert Tilsley used to wear. I was so frightened I just couldn't move a muscle.

Furiously I nudged Don and whispered to him that

there was a strange man in the bedroom. But I didn't get much response. This figure seemed very relaxed and at home and slowly he began to take his jacket and then his shirt off. I know it sounds silly, but then he started to take his braces off. I thought, 'My God!' and I really forced myself to dig Don as hard as I could in the ribs and shout. At the sound of my shout this figure just went all sort of wobbly like a dream sequence in a film and gradually faded away.

I was terrified. I broke out into this awful sweat. Don never saw a thing, of course, and was highly under-whelmed by my whole ghostly experience.

A few days later I was in the back garden hanging my washing out when I got chatting to our new neighbour. She said, 'She were never happy you know.' I pricked my ears up and got the whole story about how the man of the house we were living in had committed suicide. He was an ambu-lance driver, so that accounted for the bag. After that I always felt a shade uneasy there. I never believed in ghosts until then.

My other daughter said that one night she woke up to find more than one person sitting chanting round her bed – a man with a long beard and some others – and it was as though they were praying for someone. And our dog would never go up those steps.

Yet for all that the house had a nice feel. We lived there for quite a few years. In fact we only sold it when we moved to Manchester.

I always liked singing but to be honest I never really

wanted the pressure of having to make it a career when you simply *have* to get up on stage to sing. Emotionally I paid quite a price during those early years of marriage. Travelling miles and miles across the country and then arriving to find a bunch of stuffy committee men looking down their noses at you and telling you what recognised acts they had paid off from their grotty little club can be quite daunting.

Some of them were like little Hitlers. Strangely, some of the people that treated us the worst were miners. Not all of them – but some of them would be dreadful to work for. It was not unusual to be stuffed into a cleaning cupboard full of mops and cleaning fluid to prepare for going on. And this was at a time when they were campaigning really strongly for better working conditions!

They worked hard for their money and they just expected everyone who worked for them, who they thought was getting really well paid, to get on and entertain without any special treatment.

Sometimes when you jump up on stage to do your best to entertain a crowd of half-drunk punters who don't really listen, it's hard. It is very hard to look jolly and take over the club with your voice and personality when you are really fed up to the back teeth with the whole idea of entertaining.

I had a lesson from a real old pro along those lines one night. I won't name him because it might upset him, but he was a club comic and a very good one. One night I was appearing with him when he got a message to say that his brother had been killed in the Army. It was broken to him right at the club shortly before he was supposed to go on.

I thought, 'God, poor bloke, he'll never be able to go on and do this act now.' He went out into the car park and he was absolutely heartbroken, you could see him just wandering around the cars and sobbing. But he managed to pull himself together and slowly he went up on stage for his act. As he picked up the microphone there was a total transformation. He went down an absolute storm. He had all the women in the place doing the can-can, he was fantastic. You would have thought he hadn't a care in the world.

It puzzled me. On one level I admired him as a real professional, but on another I felt it wasn't quite normal to be able to suppress your emotions quite so successfully. I couldn't have done what he did in those circumstances to save my life.

For me a lot of the pressure came in those early days from the fact that I was only doing the clubs at the weekend. I could hardly ever do them in the week because of the kids. But if I did perform regularly it was never as bad on my nerves. If I had all the week off my anxiety had time to build up and it was almost like starting all over again.

There are so many ups and downs in the show business fourth division that it's hard to keep a handle on your feelings. But I think one night in a club in Sandiacre, near Nottingham, rates as one of my most unusual experiences. I didn't have a booking that weekend and Don and I had been sitting by the telephone hoping an agent would get a cancellation so we would be able to rush out and earn some much-needed money.

You could get a phone call and a job right up until

eight o'clock because if an act failed to turn in or rang in sick they wouldn't get the message until the club opened at seven. We would sit there all ready to go, hoping for the call. We used to ring a few agents if we were really keen.

That night the call came to rush off down the M1 to Sandiacre. But what I didn't know was that the act that had let them down was a drag act!

Don decided not to tell me about this so when I arrived with my stiletto heels and sequinned dress they thought I was a man dressed up as a woman. They were wondering which toilet I was going to use. Don thought it was a huge joke.

6
Acting Apprenticeship

I never had a plan to become famous. I didn't go off for secret acting lessons or plot desperately late into the night to get myself the best acting job in Britain. Nobody really believes me when I say it, but it just happened.

Sometimes I still pinch myself to think that at 31 I was living in a council house with four young kids and an electrician husband. And I have gone from that without a single acting lesson to play Vera Duckworth, who seems to be loads of people's favourite character in the most popular show in Britain.

I'm not ambitious, really, but I always did want the best for the family and Don kept encouraging me to get on.

I only started doing work as an extra on television because of the money you could make. Back in the early 1970s you could make £10 for a day standing round in the studio. I thought that sounded easier money than travelling round to a nightclub for half the night and singing your heart out.

Every year the clubs in Yorkshire used to have a command performance at the Opera House in Blackpool. The auditions to get on that show were very important because to be on that command performance was a great honour, and it could do you a lot of good. I had been asked by an agent from Dewsbury to go along to the auditions at Rotherham which were being run by ATS in Leeds who were based at the famous City Varieties. I was told to be there at eight o'clock and I found that they were putting all their acts on first.

In a club, the later it gets the harder it gets, because the audience gets tired. Often they've had a bit to drink and they start talking and stop listening. That night they were pushing all the acts from other agents to the back. I was sitting watching, waiting for my turn, which never seemed to come.

Gradually I was getting more and more annoyed about this. It took me until 10 o'clock to reach boiling point and then, when there was still no sign of me going on, I stormed into the office of Claud Hunter from ATS and gave him the sort of earful that Vera Duckworth would have been justifiably proud of.

I was really fed up and I told him exactly why at the top of my voice. We had set off really early because we knew there were lots of acts to fit in. Don finished work early and I had managed to find someone to look after the kids and we rushed at full speed down to Rotherham. We got there at 6.30 to make sure we were well in time for the eight o'clock start. But we were still sitting there, like a pair of lemons, at 10 o'clock at night.

I said to Claud Hunter, 'When am I on? I have been sitting waiting all this time. I've left my children at home. I think it's a disgusting way to treat people.'

There was a bloke standing with him in black leather, one of the acts. I turned to him and found out when he was on and then I said, 'Right, I'm going on straight after you.' They said, 'Oh, no. We've got a running order.'

Then I started shouting a bit. 'Listen,' I yelled as loud as I could manage. 'I'm on after him. Have you got that?' I stormed out, still shaking with anger and I told Don, 'We're on after him.' 'Yes,' he said. 'I heard.'

In the end I carried on so much that Claud Hunter's sidekick said, 'Are you in Equity?' As luck would have it I had just filled in all my Equity forms because I fancied doing some of this extra work. I reached to show him my Equity card and I couldn't find it so I emptied my bag out on his table. You should have seen the look on his face.

After my card appeared Hunter's assistant said, 'We have auditions tomorrow at the City Varieties with the actor and writer Colin Welland for a new play he has written about a tailoring strike in Leeds. We need some Leeds people and I think there might be a small part in it for you.'

Colin Welland's mother-in-law had been involved in a big strike in Leeds and he had written a powerful play about it. Many of the country's big tailoring factories were in Leeds and the workers there were very badly paid. All they wanted was a shilling an hour rise.

So I went to the Varieties the day after and Colin Welland seemed to quite like me. I didn't quite know what to expect. He was there with the director. I remember thinking, 'I mustn't be shy and dry up,' so I was a little bit cheeky as we chatted. I think they thought I was another Irma, from *Coronation Street*.

But it was a very expensive play to stage and apparently it was proving very difficult to get the BBC to agree the finance. We got chatting and then he said he had a part in another play called *Kisses at Fifty* that might suit me. Bill Maynard was the main character in that, and James Hazeldine, who is nowadays in *London's Burning*, was in it as well. Michael Apted directed.

It was one of Bill Maynard's first big parts after he stopped being a comedian and switched more to acting. He was playing a man facing the change of life. His fiftieth birthday was having a real effect upon him and he looked like going right off the rails. I might not have understood it that well at the time, but now I know exactly how he feels.

After I was registered with the agency it seemed people were actually thinking about me as an actress! Before we even got as far as recording *Kisses at Fifty* I was asked to audition for a commercial for Alan Parker. It was for Cadbury's Cookies and they wanted a mother and child. I took the little lad next door because Graham was too young. But his mum and dad came from Glasgow so he had a strong Scots accent, so although they picked me I was given another child.

In the end it was down to me and another woman.

She had done a lot of television work but she spoke very correct Queen's English and I think my authentic Yorkshire tones made Alan Parker choose me and the little boy from Barnsley.

I was just a typical Yorkshire mum, which fortunately wasn't too hard for me. I just had to try to coax my son out from under the bed with a biscuit after a disappointing day at football. I had to say, 'Come on, Tim. I'm sure all goalies let in ten goals at some time in their career.' It seemed to strike a chord with people, and quite a few things came in for me after that.

The week after that I was asked to audition for Barry Hines, who wrote *Kes*. The second play he wrote was *Speech Day*, with a similar theme to *Kes*, starring Brian Glover again and set in a comprehensive school. They offered me a part in that as well.

That play was made in Sheffield in a huge block of flats. Not quite the glamorous location I would have picked. I had already been in enough grotty flats to last me a lifetime, but I was still excited by the opportunity. They put all this black stuff in my hair to make it look as though it was dyed and all my roots wanted doing and make me look really downtrodden.

I couldn't believe that all these people wanted me to act. In those days I was generally more worried about getting the kids' dinner money right than swotting up on acting. But then I suppose I've been acting all my life.

Never in my wildest dreams did I think I would be able to move on to acting for real. Yet it slowly dawned on me that there was no magic about this acting business. I watched and I learned and I realised that if I relaxed at least I could be myself with my natural voice, which was what they seemed to want.

On 1 October 1972 I set off to stay in the Royal Victoria Hotel in Sheffield to film *Speech Day*. I had hardly stayed away from home and Don and the kids before, and I was just so excited I thought I wouldn't be able to speak, let alone act. I was playing a character called Mrs Warboys.

It was just magical. Of course most of the time I was hanging around. That is par for the course, I learned later, but I didn't mind a bit. I was still too high up on cloud nine about the fantastic hotel room I'd slept in to be worried about nerves or anything.

When I first saw Brian Glover I thought he was the scenery shifter. He was so big and muscly I didn't think he could possibly be an actor. When I found out who he was and that I was playing his wife, I started to panic. The idea of getting into bed with him was mind-blowing. He was going bald on top but he had this thin white hair that looked as if it had been powdered.

His head was like a baby's bottom. I said I would like to play noughts and crosses on the top and I don't think he was too impressed. I don't think he quite knew what to make of me. The wardrobe lady took me into the back and put this nightie on me and, honest to God, I was much more nervous about the prospect of having to get into bed with him than I was worried about acting.

I think that deep down I knew even then that I would be able to act. At first I was terrified and I got through on raw nerves. It was hard because one minute I would be on the phone to Don talking about something to do with the kids and then I'd scream, 'Don, I've got to go to work now, I can't be worrying about anything to do with the home just now,' which was an awful thing to say. But you do have to concentrate.

He would be talking on about some bill that had come in and I would say, 'Yes, I'll sort it out when I get home,' but I was standing there in a red wig waiting to go into a room to pretend to be somebody else. Mind you, it was very difficult for Don as well because he had to take time off work when I was away so quite a bit of what I earned had to go on paying for that.

I had been acting all my life, really, like a lot of people. Hiding my feelings and struggling to disguise my nerves was nothing new to me. Half of acting is confidence, and in my life I have found that I have to act more off screen than on.

All my scenes with Brian were in that miserable council flat in Sheffield. It wasn't that much different to me than doing Avon calling or going round with my wigs. That was just as much acting to me. Everybody acts. Lots of people do it all the time. And our Graham was the same age at that time as the kid who was my son in the play.

Barry Hines spent quite a lot of time asking me about our Graham and my ambitions for him. I just said,

'As long as he is happy and gets a job he enjoys doing, then that's all right with me.'

Speech Day was all very true to life. It was a wonderful play. The theme was about how the clever kids who don't really need that much help tend to get a lot of the attention at school while the kids with a problem, who do need help, are often ignored.

Barry had been a teacher and he knew what happened in schools. I played a mother who didn't really give her younger son enough help at home. He wasn't unintelligent but I just used to send him out all the time. It taught me a lot about the power of television because a lot of people recognised me and got the message.

Then later the same month I went down to London to the BBC studios at White City to film *Kisses at Fifty*. Bill Maynard and Marjorie Yates were the stars, and I was playing Enid.

This was a very important role for Bill Maynard. He had been a really big comedy star but then a lot of problems had upset his career and he was starting again almost as a straight actor. He was very good; I learned a lot just from looking at him. The play went on to win a BAFTA award and Bill went on to star in another comedy series with a crazy character called Selwyn Froggitt. He always said how important *Kisses at Fifty* was to his career and he offered all the people who had been in the play roles in his new television series.

Kisses at Fifty was like being in a dream. Me, Sylvia Butterfield, being an actress at the BBC! I kept thinking, Any minute now I'm going to wake up in bed in Leeds with a load of nappies to wash.

I had to go off on the train to London on my own. Can you imagine my feelings on the platform in Leeds with my kids waving me off? It felt weird and unreal and exciting all at the same time. I had to keep pinching myself to make sure it was the real me it was all happening to.

We had digs in Shepherd's Bush, and they were awful. You would just be dropping off to sleep and a mouse would run across your head. The BBC used to pay fantastic expenses, more than the fee. Then they steered us towards these awful digs.

Another Northern actress called Christine Buckley was with me, and we travelled across London together. Now the Tube was a bit of a shock for me, I'd never seen anything quite like it. But I could follow Christine and do just what she did. She had a scarf round her. We were going into London from Shepherd's Bush one day and as a train came I just got sort of swept by the crowd onto it. I saw the scarf waving in the air away from me and I thought, 'My God, we've got separated.'

When I reached the other end I waited at the top of the escalator for Christine, and she never came. After about 45 minutes I plucked up courage and asked this big coloured guard, 'When is the next train from Shepherd's Bush?'

He knew I had been standing there for ages and he looked at me as though I was mad. He said, 'Lady, there are hundreds of trains.' Eventually I did manage to find my way back to the rehearsal rooms at North Acton and

Christine was sitting there with that blasted scarf around her neck. I must have been looking at someone else's scarf all the time. I was so green. But you don't understand Tubes when you've never been on one.

I wince when I think of how I was in those days. I was so naive. One of the biggest television shows of the day was *Dr Finlay's Casebook*, which starred Bill Simpson. But I had never watched it because I was always singing in the clubs.

So when this chap started talking to me one day at the North Acton rehearsal rooms I didn't know him from a bar of soap. Somebody introduced me to this chap called Bill and I just said, 'Oh, hello. What do you do?' It's a stupid thing to say, but I was so green then. He said, 'I work behind the bar, but it's my night off.' I bought him a drink because I thought, 'For once I'm earning good money and he is only a barman.'

In the end he said, 'I'm Bill Simpson.' I said. 'Yes, you told me.' He began to find his joke wearing a bit thin with someone who really didn't recognise him and finally, a little exasperated, he said, 'I'm Doctor Finlay,' and at last the penny dropped. I learned a lesson from that. Never ask someone what they do, because it obviously upset him that I didn't know who he was.

The BBC was celebrating its fiftieth anniversary while we were recording that play, and the studios were absolutely packed with famous faces recording big shows with really big stars in. I just kept pinching myself to make sure I wasn't dreaming as I walked around.

Once I was in the canteen and I found myself queueing up with Robert Wagner, Morecambe and Wise. By the time I got to the till I had only picked up an orange. It just mesmerised me, I couldn't believe I was there. Me, Sylvia Butterfield from Torre Mount, Leeds, a club act from nowhere who had managed to get a part in a play on the BBC! It was like I was in a trance. Little Ronnie Corbett was in front, Lulu behind me. All the Goons were there – Michael Bentine, Peter Sellers and so on. Everywhere I looked there was a famous celebrity. It was unbelievable.

When I got to the table I still only had my orange. The other people in the play were laughing. They said, 'You can't just have an orange.' But by then I was too nervous to go back. I didn't want to show myself up in front of all those famous people.

That was the start of it all – a complete change in my life. The next year I got a part in another Colin Welland play, the one that everyone remembers – *Leeds United*, about the strike. Lynne Perrie from *Coronation Street* was in that and I already knew her a little from the clubs.

It was a very political play, all about the dreadful conditions in tailoring factories. That was something I knew a lot more about than Colin Welland, of course, and I was proud to be in it. Mind you, we should have had a medical check-up after it was over. They had us marching round the streets of Leeds for days on end.

My mother would have been horrified at the

thought of striking and demonstrating on the streets. And we had to go down to Belle Vue to be filmed demonstrating at a real rally. It was a serious Left-wing occasion with Vanessa Redgrave in full flow.

I will always remember the instruction on our script from the BBC. It said, 'Dress down, in something you might get from C&A.' I was shocked. I had never been able to afford clothes from C&A. I thought that was where the posh people shopped! You had to pay cash at C&A. I used to buy all our clothes on tick out of the catalogues.

Gradually I was learning that there might be more to this show business lark than I had thought. It had always simply been a way to bring a bit more money into the house. I had never even considered it as a real career, me being an actress. That didn't happen to ordinary people like me.

I got the train over the Pennines to Granada in January 1974 to work on a show called *How's Your Father*, and then I rushed back to appear in a sketch with the great Les Dawson at Yorkshire TV in Leeds. Not every famous person you meet in television is as nice as you imagine, but Les was every bit as genuine and cuddly in the flesh as he was on the screen. I was a total nobody appearing on his show, *Sez Les*, which was very big at the time, and he treated me as though I was a film star they had flown in from America.

We were doing this sketch where he had to come next to me and clown around a bit and he could see I was in pain. I explained that the bending was hurting my back and he switched things around so I didn't have to bend at all. I never forget little acts of kindness like that and we remained friends until his recent tragic death.

7
Enter Vera Duckworth

Vera Duckworth made her first brief appearance in *Coronation Street* in July 1974 when she started work at the Mark Brittain Warehouses which were built on the site of the old raincoat factory. My memory of actually landing a job in *Coronation Street* is a fuzzy blur now. It really was an astonishing experience. I found myself mixing with a lot of people who were household names across the country, who had been coming into my home twice a week for years. I think I was so star-struck I can't really remember much about that very first time.

Everyone was very nice and helpful, of course, but I really had to steel myself to go in there. After all *Coronation Street* is something special. I had grown up watching Ken Barlow and Annie Walker. Our family all used to sit round on Mondays and Wednesdays as regular as Sunday lunchtime.

Like any viewers I just thought of them as real people. There was a warmth and an accessibility about the programme that always made it one of my favourites. That's why I had queued up years before to sit on the knee of Dennis Tanner. I was just as impressed meeting the actor Philip Lowrie, who was charming.

But when I walked into the *Street* studios for the first time I was already acting. I felt that from the first moment I had to show them I was capable, and you can't act capable if you behave like a mouse, can you? So I would grit my teeth, switch on my most confident smile and stride into action as though I'd just called in from the Royal Shakespeare Company.

I would hide my nerves inside and get through the day as quickly and as best as possible. I've found out later, of course, that lots of other people went through just the same sort of anxiety. But I didn't know that at the time.

All the most established actors went out of their way to be kind. I remember Bill Roache putting his arm round me and saying how well he thought a particularly emotional scene had gone. He never knew how grateful I was for that gesture of support.

This was a time when Ken Barlow had been offered a job in the warehouse. Before then in the story he had led an objection by the people of Coronation Street to the introduction of extra traffic which was upsetting their peace and quiet. Regular viewers will know that extra traffic has featured in another major story in the Street almost twenty years later, but then life – and with it *Coronation Street* – does tend to travel full circle if you wait long enough.

Anyway, as Vera appeared for the very first time she found that the warehouse manager had been so impressed by the way Ken spoke up and handled himself that he had offered him a junior executive's job. Ken was until then a dedicated teacher, but he liked the sound of the extra money and the challenge of a position in commerce.

Just as Ken and Vera joined there was union trouble. Vera was naturally enough in the front line as spokeswoman with Ivy. We were campaigning for unionisation, but the management were dead against it.

What I didn't realise until later was that *Coronation Street* characters have backgrounds and histories all carefully prepared for them by a talented team of writers and storyline experts. Vera Duckworth might not be real, but she was born on 3 September 1937. She came into the world in Moss-side, Manchester, in an air raid, so she hardly had a silver spoon in her mouth.

Vera's mother, Amy Burton – who was to arrive in Weatherfield years later – had to give birth at home because the hospital was full. But from her earliest beginnings Vera was never an easy person. My fictional mother, so the *Street* historians tell me, went into labour in Marks & Spencer's when she was queueing for cheap cake and clothing.

Vera went to Moss-side Secondary Modern School but she spent most of her time playing truant and meeting boys in amusement arcades. When I learned that gem from Vera's master file in the depths of Granada I started to wonder just how much research into my real life those clever scriptwriters had done.

As the fictional story goes, Vera was twenty when

she met Jack Duckworth on a fairground in Blackpool. He was in charge of the dodgems and she was looking for a ride. He took her away from her mother and they really fell for each other. Her mother insisted they got married for decency's sake and they first lived in Gas Street, Weatherfield, not far from Coronation Street.

Exciting as my first appearances on *Coronation Street* were, it didn't seem that they would lead to anything. I never imagined for a minute that I had the remotest chance of becoming a regular on the show. That year I went on to make a string of brief appearances.

I just thought it was an interesting sideline that brought a few more pounds into the house. But it never paid enough for me to stop doing other jobs. In fact sometimes the two worlds collided with almost disastrous consequences.

I got the chance to appear on a new comedy show called *The Wheeltappers and Shunters Social Club* as a waitress. At the time I was working in a hair lacquer and toothpaste factory. When I got the call there was no time to ask properly for time off. I just told the supervisor, 'I've got to go. I've left a pan of stew on the stove.'

I did the show and a few weeks later May, the supervisor, called me into her office and told me that she had seen a waitress on this TV show that was just my double. 'Really,' I said in mock astonishment. I think I really was learning how to act by this time.

I did a thing at Yorkshire TV called *Our Kid* with

Ken Platt. I only had a small part but they wanted me to have a big cleavage. Well, I've never been well off in that department. They decided to make the best of what I'd got by strapping me up in sticky tape and shading in with lots of heavy make-up. Why they didn't just hire an actress with big boobs if that's what they wanted I'll never know.

I was just somebody's girlfriend who walked in with a plate of food and said, 'Here's your dinner.' They made me look really tarty with red hair and loads of make-up. Then when I got back in the dressing room Don had to get this sticky tape off me, and it tore all my skin. I was in agony.

I was still doing the clubs, of course, and when it started to register with people that they weren't just listening to Liz Dawn sing but getting to meet Vera Duckworth from *Coronation Street* into the bargain my money started to go up.

We had some good nights in the clubs. Newcastle was always one of my favourite bookings. The White House, Newcastle, was terrific – they used to charge admission of £5 even in those days, and put a real show on. I went there once with a comedian called George King, who appeared on TV's *Comedians*, and Tony Christie, who was very big at the time with records in the charts, was top of the bill.

George was compere and he did a bit himself before I went on. Somehow everything clicked, and I've hardly ever gone down better. The audience were really joining in and enjoying themselves. But by the time Tony Christie came on I'm afraid a lot of them were half cut. He had a seven-piece band. But as soon as he went into his big hit, 'Amarillo', he found half the audience was on stage joining in. It completely ruined his act. With those audiences it didn't matter who you were. If they were in the mood to take over you'd better just get out of the way.

It was in that part of the country where I experienced a total contrast – the two different ends of show business – in two consecutive days. First we went up to a champagne Variety Club sponsored race meeting at Gosforth Park. We were with Tony Booth and Pat Phoenix. We were driven to the course in a Rolls Royce and given the most fantastic VIP treatment you could imagine. After a while I almost started to think I was important. We finished the day at a big banquet at the Newcastle Council House. It was a fabulous day.

The following lunchtime I was booked to do a club. When we got there I thought there was something odd about the place. It didn't dawn on me straight away it was that there were no women there.

Until I went into the dressing room, that was. There was a woman in there who announced, 'I'm on before you.' I said, 'Oh, are you?' But she was upset because she had forgotten her music. I offered to lend her one of mine and she went out with 'Freedom Come, Freedom Go'. But I still didn't realise that she was going to do a striptease instead of sing! At last the penny dropped and I realised I had been booked to appear with strippers!

Don found the concert secretary, who had conveniently forgotten to explain just what sort of a do this was. Don said to this bloke, 'There is no way Liz is appearing with strippers,' because I was in *Coronation Street* then. But I said to Don, 'I've never walked out on a club yet, and I don't want to start now.' I said, 'I'm going to go on. And then I'm off.' And I did a spot as quickly as possible. I sang four or five songs and did 20 minutes and told them that was that.

They came up afterwards and asked me to go on again, but I refused. These clubs, particularly the ones in the north east, absolutely revel in telling you what well-known acts they have paid off. So we told them that for the first time we were paying them off. They could keep their money and I was not going on again. They looked very surprised, but after a wonderful day the day before I just couldn't face going on stage in front of a load of men who had really only come to leer at the strippers.

Things still weren't easy. I was still a housewife first, and often the practical difficulties of trying to fit work in with my responsibilities at home had me almost tearing my hair out. When I did *The Wheeltappers* they used to film it at a real club in Manchester at night and by the time we had finished it was too late for a through train back to Leeds. I used to end my day half asleep on a slow train back to Huddersfield and Don would pick me up at the station after midnight.

I went on to play a character in a very funny play by Alan Bennett, directed by Stephen Frears no less, called

Sunset Across the Bay. Then I was Mrs Higgins with young Mr Frears directing again in *Daft As A Brush* with Lynn Redgrave and Jonathan Pryce in the cast. I was starting to rub shoulders with some very famous people. I remember being in a caravan with Lynn Redgrave, chatting together as we had our make-up done.

The first time I ever wore a curly wig on screen was playing a prison officer in Granada's *Crown Court*. I did that for years. I was in the very first one and although it was not the most demanding of roles it was a great steady income. Almost every time they had a woman defendant they had me as a woman prison officer standing grimly beside her.

To me the important thing about *Crown Court* was the quality of the actors they used to get in. I think my favourite was Joan Hickson, who went on to be so popular as Miss Marple. She was accused of some dreadful crime. To watch her work was an education. I used to watch the cameras, listen to the director and try to learn something new in every episode. I always joke that *Crown Court* was my RADA – free drama training on the job.

It was all very nice, of course, but I was still rushing back to look after the children in between and I was in and out of ordinary jobs as well. When you're young you think you can do anything.

But a shadow fell across my world at this time, because my mother became very ill. I stopped singing in the clubs for a while and got a job in Gibbs's hair lacquer and toothpaste factory so I could see her every day.

The world of the hospitals is another world, isn't it? I have never found it easy to cope with illness. I hated seeing my mother laid low. I will never forget being told the awful truth that she was not going to get better. She had had an operation and been fitted with a colostomy bag and she was really angry. She said, 'Look what they have done to me.'

I was just on the way out of hospital and this young doctor came up and said, 'Can I have a word with you?' As soon as I heard that, I knew it was going to be dreadful news. I was in shock straight away. I could see his mouth opening and shutting but I couldn't make sense of what was coming out. It was terrible. I couldn't walk, I couldn't talk, I couldn't even think. He just said, real matter of fact, 'Your mother has between three and six months to live.'

I went to the bus stop with Joyce, a friend of mine, and I looked so awful she took me for a drink. They had to take me in a pub to revive me. I had a large brandy and felt a bit better. I had never been in pubs for years at the time, but I'm afraid I've been in plenty since. The responsibility of me being the only one who had this awful knowledge was dreadful. I kept thinking over and over again, 'My mother's going to die and I don't know what to do.'

In the end I rang my auntie up at work. There was certainly a better way of doing it, but I was not thinking that straight.

After that I really learned to act because I had to

play a part with my mother, pretending that she really was going to get better. And she was probably acting with me. I'm sure she really knew that she was not going to recover.

She came out of hospital and I used to see her every day, in fact I neglected my kids for her. I just thought, 'She is my mother,' and everything else had to take a back seat for a while. Nothing else was that important. I just thought, 'While she is alive, I will be there.'

I know it sounds awful, but she had a bottle of sherry in the cupboard and I often used to take a drink out of it to help myself to put on a brave face for my mother. She must have noticed, because there was nobody sharper than my mother, but she never let on.

Life can be very cruel because this happened just at the time when she could have taken things a little easier. She had just been made forewoman so there was someone else to man those Hoffman presses at last.

She was suffering from cancer of the bowel, and when I had an interview for *Daft As A Brush* I said, 'I won't go, I'll stay with you, mum.'

She wouldn't hear of it. She said, 'No. You go. I'll be all right until you come back.' But I still didn't want to leave her because I felt so sad and guilty when I went. I was only away about one and a half hours, but I still felt guilty. It doesn't matter how much you do, you never think you've done enough.

My mother died in April 1975, aged fifty-seven. She had lived for another fourteen months after the doctor made his grim prediction. It was such a terrible blow I don't think I've ever fully recovered from it. My mother was so important to me, so alive, so vital. She had always been there for me.

She was always the one who kept everybody going, she provided the lift until then. She was the anchor in our family. Her illness seemed to go on and on and on. Cancer can be so cruel. After she died I didn't organise the funeral or anything, my dad did it. It left such an awful gaping hole in my life. For ages I felt as though someone had pushed me out of an aeroplane with no parachute. I was lost, completely lost.

I think in a peculiar way that is why I like to go round hospices even today. When I walk in someone can be really, really ill and I can use Vera's popularity to give them a lift. For a split second at least they forget all their pain and agony and have a tiny relief. That is an enormous privilege.

That was the start of troubles for me. The pain has never really gone away. I am glad she saw me get into *Coronation Street*. But I could have done so much for her if she had lived, taken her on holidays and all sorts.

The most heart-breaking moment for me came afterwards, when all my mother's things from the hospital were brought round in a big bag. There was a knock at the door and they were there with her nightie and things. It just seemed so hard and brutal.

When I look back I think that my mother had more life in her fifty-seven years than some people have who live until they are ninety. She had a really happy life. People liked her, she was always popular. Life was always fun when she was around. She worked so hard, but she enjoyed herself as well. She loved to go out to the club with my dad, or go off on trips.

It was terribly soon after my mother died that I went to Granada to be in *Green Hill Pals*. It couldn't have been less suitable for my state of mind at the time because it was a very sombre play about old soldiers going back to visit the First World War battlefields. I seemed to spend weeks filming in graveyards in Belgium. Every other grave seemed to have on it someone's name and then these tragically young ages – sixteen, seventeen or eighteen. You can imagine how I felt. It was probably one of the lowest times of my life.

Jimmy Jewell was the star and he was such a kind, gentle man. There was one poor chap, an extra in the film, who found the grave of his brother. It was like a body blow to him and Jimmy was very upset as well. He did his level best to comfort the man. Those graves brought home to all of us the crazy inhumanity of war.

I had never been abroad before. I had awful tension at the back of my neck. I was very worried about that part. It was one of the most expensive things Granada had done at the time and there were dire warnings on the script against taking too long over the production, so there was somehow an extra responsibility. I was the only woman in it and I was going over there with eighteen old men and a bus driver. I wasn't really up to it emotionally, but as it went on I just found myself swept along by the whole enterprise. And I was on tablets for my nerves.

When I came back they asked me to do more waitressing on *Wheeltappers and Shunters*. I thought, 'My God, I've just done all that proper acting and they want me to be a barmaid!' But it was Granada, and it was there that producer June Howson said they had a speaking part for me in *Crown Court*. She explained it was a challenging part, but it would mean giving up being the prison officer.

The role was Bedelia Conroy, landlady of the Feathers Hotel, Fulchester, and I loved absolutely every minute. It gave me the chance to be loud and blowsy. She was a great character and I'll always believe that it was the powers that be at Granada that spotted me in that part of bossy Bedelia who decided they would develop that sort of character for me and realise the potential of Vera Duckworth.

I knew Bedelia Conroy was something special. I learned every line of that *Crown Court* episode, my part and everyone else's as well. When I went in to the read through I was shivering with fear, but they told me just to use my own voice and relax. I was a lot younger then and even verging on being slim and attractive, and one of the actors, John Ronane, thought I was wonderful for putting on such an authentic Northern accent. When he realised I was using my real voice I don't think he was quite so impressed.

The set was so real that you felt you were really in court. Patrick Troughton, Sylvia Kay and Maria Charles were the stars. They were very good and I learned a lot by watching them. I had a part to really get my teeth into at last. I loved that part. I knew it off by heart because I lived it. I just wanted to learn that part so well.

I suppose I was very unprofessional, and I soon learned that deep down nobody has that much confidence, but I wanted to show all these highly trained and professional actors that I could do it too. I put some new boots on even though you couldn't see my feet on screen, and I had my hair done and everything. I heard an actor say, 'She's good,' and I realised that people were laughing at my voice. They didn't realise I really talked like that, they thought I was just good at putting on the Yorkshire accent.

Patrick Troughton was such a good actor and he was really nice. I liked him because he had no airs and graces about him, he was straight and down to earth. He used to carry his script around in a carrier bag. I thought that was great because I had seen actors wandering round at Granada who only had a few lines and they were carrying their scripts around in briefcases.

Then I worked with Ron Moody in an episode of a series called *Village Hall*. It was election day and I was a voter who came in at the last minute trying to squeeze my vote in. He was the returning officer. Again I learned a lot from watching him. I was so in awe of him I could hardly speak at first, but he really put me at my ease.

Alan Parker was a lovely chap. He used me again in a very funny commercial for Formica. It was the middle of summer when Don and I drove down to London for that, and it was a baking hot day. The car overheated on the M1 and we were left standing there for two hours while we got it going again. London was heaving with tourists and we went round to Alan Parker's office. He had just done *Bugsy Malone* and he had a really smart office. We had to wait in there for two hours to get in, and we had an appointment.

On the way to the hotel a wasp got into the car and Don said, 'Put your foot on it,' and I did but it crawled up my leg right to the top and stung me! We were in the middle of a horrendous traffic jam and we pulled into a garage and I leaped out onto the forecourt and started ripping my jeans off. It's a wonder I didn't get a part in something more interesting than a commercial.

This garage man came running out and said, 'Madam, you cannot do that in my garage.' We found some stuff in the end to spray on and calm down the bite, but by the time we got to the hotel my nerves were frazzled.

We'd been told to order what we wanted at the hotel and I was starving so I rang room service and ordered a steak. A while later this waiter arrived with the biggest cheesecake I'd ever seen. It could only happen to me. It was a perfectly crazy end to a crazy day.

The commercial was funny. It had me as a pushy wife going into a shop with a weedy little husband and a lie detector. When all the lights flashed we realised that he was trying to palm us off with a cheap substitute for Formica. Apparently this advert had a very good effect on sales. It also had quite a good effect on my career because Larry Grayson rang wanting me to star in his new TV series for London Weekend Television.

Larry was marvellous – so outrageous and full of life. He wanted me as Dot the neighbour, and I went down and played the part in a special. Again, I was playing a larger than life version of myself but I didn't mind that. It was good fun for once and the money paid for quite a lot of nappies.

Larry wanted me to do the series, but then came the most amazing experience when Granada decided the factory was going to be a regular feature of *Coronation Street* and they wanted to see much more of Vera Duckworth. Granada decided this factory girl with a big mouth was to be a regular character.

This was a great chance for me and I should have been elated, but somehow I wasn't. In truth I was still desperately grieving for my mother. When you have watched somebody you really love die it has a funny effect upon you. I became obsessed with the doctors. I would drag the kids there on the slightest excuse, and I was convinced I was going to die myself.

I can remember dragging my case to King's Cross after doing the Larry Grayson show and thinking, 'I don't care if I live or die.' I really was depressed. I thought, 'When I get home I'm going to throw all these pills down the toilet.' I just didn't care any more. I thought, 'I am going out for a drink and I'm going to have too much.'

I got home on the Saturday morning and I just tipped all my bottles of pills down the loo. That was my lowest ebb. All the Valium was washed away. I had a good doctor who would do anything to avoid giving you pills, but I needed them when he prescribed them.

8
My Big Break

After everything I was on the verge of my biggest break. Not only did it seem that I had actually arrived as a real-life television actress, which still took a bit of believing, I can tell you, but also I had been given a choice of two fantastic roles, co-starring with Larry Grayson on what was the big new comedy show of the day, and getting a long run in *Coronation Street*.

I was gobsmacked, for want of a better word. I did agonise over the decision but in the end it was no contest. *Coronation Street* had been part of my life as I was growing up, and the chance to join that family of famous faces was just too good to pass up.

I don't want to sound boastful but it somehow was a bigger thing when anyone joined the *Street* in those days. The cast was very well established and had been fairly stable for a long period. Nowadays, with the faster pace of scenes and three episodes a week, there are more people coming and going every time. But in those days joining *Coronation Street* was really something incredibly special. At least that is how it felt to me.

Vera had popped up quite a few times by then, and I was happy doing the part. She has never been a million miles from the real me. The name came from Harry Kershaw's wife, who was called Vera. Harry was one of the most important writers and producers *Coronation Street* ever had. He carefully moulded the original Vera so I know I will always owe him a great debt. He saw something in me that he could use, and I will always be very grateful.

By the time I became a semi sort of regular I was quite relaxed and a bit less in awe of the whole *Street* experience. Everyone was very nice, but they all had their own parts to concern themselves with. I used to sit quietly in the dressing room trying to get it all right in my head and then I would be called for a scene. I never had much to say to the rest of the cast. It was just a job to me like all the hundreds of others I'd had.

I enjoyed it. I thought it was nice that I could come home and talk about the people in *Coronation Street*, but by then I was no longer in awe of the other actors. I didn't think they were any better than me. I was not an extra waiting around to be given a part. I did other roles.

For quite a few years I didn't have a proper contract like the real regulars. I was just hired for three weeks at a time so I knew it was easy for me to be dropped. Sometimes I was in more than the real regulars were, but I never had the security of a contract for years. I was always frightened that I was going to get the sack. There was such pressure never to talk to the Press. We were always told to say, 'No comment'. It was a strain because I had been brought up to be straight and open with people. Joining *Coronation Street* sometimes felt like signing up for the secret service. I felt we needed the Press for publicity to help the programme.

But I never pushed it because I had my singing at weekends and the appeal of *Coronation Street* very quickly started to build up the following for my club act. People seemed to really like to see someone from the *Street* in their local club, and when they found out that I could sing and have a bit of fun as well then I was laughing because so were they.

But it wasn't easy in my early days in *Coronation Street*. All the other cast members seemed to have money and looks. The entrance to Granada Studios was very like the front of Pilkington's so-called Dancing School in Leeds that had such personal echoes of glamour for me. The other actors and actresses certainly looked really glamorous and self-assured. Even the extras looked like stars to me. I used to sit there with my little bag feeling that as usual I was looking a real mess because I was always in a rush.

I used to wonder, 'Are they all thinking, Who on earth is she?' They did get a girl called Paula Gregor to show me round after a while. She said, 'This is wardrobe, this is the canteen, this is Studio 6,' and so on. It was like going round a marvellous museum. I couldn't believe that after all these years I was actually on the inside looking out.

Singing kept my feet on the ground because I was still in touch with real people. If you are just with actors all day, and you have come out of drama school in the first place, there is a real danger that you are living in an unreal world.

Vera changed quite a bit in those early years. When she first appeared in 1974 she was a forceful factory girl demanding a better deal for the workers. Then in 1975 she came back and had somehow turned into a divorcee and the girlfriend of Fred Gee, who was the barman at that time. I even had a few lines once about a daughter who has certainly never been seen or heard of since.

Annie Walker, the legendary landlady of the Rovers Return, had taken on shiftless Fred Gee as her resident potman. He was played by a lovely actor called Fred Feast. Fred Gee was living in at the Rovers and, when he wasn't being run ragged by Annie, played by the legendary Doris Speed, he was lonely and in need of what's politely known as female company.

Annie graciously allowed Fred to 'entertain' in her lounge. He was granted actual permission to invite a friend round. This was an amazing breakthrough because Annie's views on morality dated back to Victorian times. But Annie was horrified when Fred's guest was me, Vera Duckworth. I'll never forget the scene when she curled her lip as only Annie Walker could and called me, 'That creature.'

I don't know exactly what she thought Fred and Vera were going to get up to, but Annie insisted on playing gooseberry all night long. It turned into a very good comedy scene. I learned an awful lot doing that beautifully written scene with Fred Feast and Doris Speed.

She said to me, 'Would you like a cup of tea, Miss Duckworth?' And I had to reply, 'It's Mrs Duckworth, actually. I'm divorced.' I think Vera was trying to forget that Jack had ever existed that night. We managed to convey the comedy of the situation thanks to some excellent writing, and it really seemed to register with the viewers. Vera, in the minds of many *Street* fans, had arrived.

At the Queen's Jubilee there was a glamorous granny competition that Vera was in, but I never found out what happened to any grandchildren I might have had. I was pestering about when the new factory was being opened, before Baldwin's. Then Baldwin's opened in 1975 and I had quite a lot of work.

I had been doing Vera in my short bursts for about four years before I met the man who was to become my husband on screen. Over the years Vera had often referred to Jack, usually with a typically choice insult, and I had always wondered what he was like.

But my first proper meeting with Bill Tarmey, who was to play idle Jack, was pure Duckworths. It was back in 1979 and our first scenes together were at Gail Potter's wedding to Brian Tilsley at St Boniface's Church, a popular *Coronation Street* location.

The very first time I actually met him was in make-up and I came out and walked down the corridor right past him. I didn't know him from Adam. Bill had done some extra work so he knew his way round.

We were only introduced outside the church.

Somebody said, 'This is Bill,' and he said, 'I'm playing Jack,' and I said, 'Oh, that's nice.' It seemed a bit funny meeting your husband like that, and I didn't quite know what I thought but he looked all right.

I soon got to know him a lot better. It was a bitterly cold day for filming and we were doing this scene where we all trooped out of the church. Somebody had brought in a heater to keep the worst of the cold off us while we were hanging around, which is how most time is spent while filming.

I was freezing so I stood right up against the heater and my Crimplene skirt kept brushing onto it, and it caught fire. I didn't notice, of course – being me, I was busy talking. But suddenly Bill grabbed me and threw me on the floor and started slapping my backside. I screamed. I thought, 'I'm sure this isn't in the script. He must have flipped.'

Bill said, 'I'm sorry, but you're on fire.' And of course we had a great laugh about that. It was a real ice-breaker between us because we both saw the funny side straight away. It was the start of what has been for me a wonderful partnership. I know the powers that be at Granada looked at Bill and me very carefully during those scenes. We were raw and untrained. We had never been near a drama school but we survived an education in one of the toughest fields of entertainment there is. And I like to think there was a spark between us that caught the eye.

At first we both found it very difficult. The level of

concentration and attention to detail in a show like *Coronation Street* is frightening. It was all complicated by the fact that this was the time of the big strike at ITV. The actual wedding ceremony had been recorded in August but the scenes outside in the cold afterwards were completed as winter began. So we had the guests arriving for the wedding and the reception in brilliant sunshine with all the guests wearing summer clothes. But it was not transmitted until 3 December when the weather was very bad.

We got away with it. I think the sight of Annie Walker dispensing free champagne was too startling to leave the viewers with time to notice the odd weather. Hilda Ogden gatecrashed the reception and finished up as washer-up, and Jack got drunk. That allowed Vera to give him an early ear-bashing that seemed to go down well. They had a real slanging match. I wish I had a fiver for every row they've had since then!

Bill always says he can put Jack in a box and leave him at the studios, but I find it is very hard for me to forget Vera like that.

Vera always seemed to be at the centre of a row. There was one memorable bust-up when all the girls in the factory thought they had won the Pools. But it turned out they hadn't, because yours truly had forgotten to post the coupon.

Jack was a taxi driver when we were first on, and that was how he picked up Bet Lynch, who became the 'other woman' in a favourite early storyline back in

1982. It began on Easter Monday when Jack wanted to spend the day boozing and canoodling with Bet rather than come home to Vera. Vera also had another man in the background, but he was only ever what they call a 'non-speaking extra'. They might have given me a boyfriend I could talk to! Viewers just saw Vera rushing off for a furtive meeting outside the pub and they had to imagine the worst.

It was very cleverly written because Vera knew that Jack had a girlfriend on the side but she didn't know the other woman was Bet, played by Julie Goodyear. So she chose Bet as someone to confide in, and she really opened her heart. It was quite moving as well as funny and it helped me to establish that Vera was not just a big mouth. There was actually a real human being behind that voice.

Eventually Jack gave himself away and the penny dropped with Vera. I really loved the scene when Vera finally found out what Jack had been up to. She went very noisily mad and dumped all his clothes in a plastic bag on the bar of the Rovers and told Bet Lynch she could have him.

There was a special irony about that scene for me because Don and I had been going through one of our more difficult periods. It's always been a very volatile marriage and we were just getting back together after almost splitting up. So as I was going into Granada and doing scenes about having an affair and discovering my husband was unfaithful, life at home was pretty lively as well.

We can sit and laugh about it now but at the time there was a lot of tension in the house. And when I did that important scene where I had to dump all Jack's belongings in the bar the make-up department had to work overtime to hide some of the evidence of our real emotions from my face.

When I look at those old episodes now I realise that scene went on for several minutes. You just don't get those long scenes any more. The pace of the show has really changed over the years. Now it is much, much quicker.

Vera moved in with Ivy to get away from faithless Jack. But Bert Tilsley, Ivy's first husband, wasn't too keen on that arrangement so they tried a bit of marriage guidance. They invited Jack round and more or less forced them back together.

One of my favourite stories was when Jack went to the video dating agency and tried to pass himself off as the mysterious Vince St Clair. That was on in May 1983, but people still write to me today about it.

Bill looked quite cool in his new identity and he carried it off really well. In the story I played the lady who turned up as his date. The director wanted me to wear a really revealing low-cut dress as Vera trying to disguise herself as a sophisticated lady calling herself Carol Munro. To give me a shock of lovely auburn hair I wore a big red wig. I think he wanted me to look like Maureen O'Hara. Some hopes! You can imagine the laughs we had with that.

Of course in the end Jack was stunned when he realised he had so carefully arranged himself a date with his own wife. Bill is such a clever actor he carried it off brilliantly.

So many things about working with Bill are really fun. The glasses Jack wears, stuck together with tape, always make me laugh. He couldn't afford to have them mended properly – it might cost him the price of a few pints. Bill did that himself; it is a nice touch.

Our screen son Terry arrived soon after that. It was a bit baffling because I was first introduced to a young actor from Sheffield called Tony Pitts. 'Here is your son Terry,' I was told, and everyone seemed very happy about the idea.

Then suddenly Tony disappeared before he was ever seen on screen and Nigel Pivaro became our son Terry. It was odd because they don't even look alike. But Tony went on to do very well as a very different young soap opera star, Archie Pitts in *Emmerdale*, and I still watch and admire his acting today.

Nigel stayed with us to build up quite a reputation as bad boy Terry. Nigel is a smashing young actor and from the start he got on really well with me and Bill. But I think he found some of our working practices a little hard to understand.

One of our very first scenes together was breakfast at the Duckworths. Because it was a longish scene in another heavy week both Bill and I, who are not the greatest learners of lines in the world, had a few little notes scattered around the breakfast table to make sure we did not forget any of our vital words.

There was a scrap of paper on the sugar bowl, I recall, and a few scrawled words on the top of the corn flakes packet and one or two others as well. Nigel, who had benefited from a rather more conventional dramatic training than Bill or yours truly, was absolutely astonished. He kept picking lines up out of the air like a magician and saying, 'I don't believe it.' Then he thought it was a bit of a laugh to pinch one or two of our memory aids. That experience certainly broke the ice in a jolly way, and the three of us have been almost as close as a real family ever since.

Poor Nigel suffered from a lot of daft bad publicity about one or two things in his past as soon as it became known that he was coming into the *Street*. I rang his mum and told her not to worry about that and promised we would make him welcome. I knew how daunting it was coming into a big show, so I was anxious to do anything I could to help. Not that Nigel really needed any assistance. He's a very talented and professional actor – and much better behaved than Terry!

9
Life at Number 9

We didn't move into Number 9 Coronation Street until August 1983. The first I knew about that was when I read it in the newspapers one Sunday morning. Don and I were at home in Morritt Avenue, Leeds, lying in bed enjoying a relaxing cup of tea and the papers as usual when we saw a big picture of Bill Tarmey and some suitcases and the story. It was quite a shock, I can tell you. But I was very pleased because it was like a sort of vote of confidence after being just on temporary contracts. Chalky White, who was played by Teddy Turner, put his house up for sale and Jack and Terry went round there to try to rent it. I really liked those scenes because Teddy was a club act like me and when he performed live he was nothing like the rather shabby figure he cut in *Coronation Street*.

He had a huge handlebar moustache, immaculate suits and shining crocodile shoes, and was a very funny comic. In real life he was more like a country squire than the occupant of No 9 Coronation Street. He was a dream to work with. At first we were just going to rent the house but then Jack had the idea we should try to buy it.

It was a great surprise to all concerned that the Duckworths actually managed to get a mortgage. Most of the residents of the *Street* had enormous reservations about their new neighbours, but Vera never let a little thing like that bother her.

Being the Duckworths, of course nothing went smoothly. We stayed again with Ivy for a spell, which caused great consternation, while the mortgage came through. Fred Gee had the keys because Chalky's house was empty so Jack persuaded Fred to let him store their furniture in there illegally.

But when the removal men came to take away Chalky's things they took our stuff away as well. This gave Vera the chance to launch another one-woman assault on idle Jack. I had to be really angry with Bill to make him sort all this out and I overdid it a bit. I gave him a shove and he cracked his head on the side of the removal van and nearly knocked himself out. It looked extra realistic, that did. Eventually we stored our things in the factory without Mike Baldwin ever finding out about it.

Once we got into No 9 I felt very relieved. I had been existing on temporary contracts, but after I took up residence in Coronation Street I got a regular contract.

After we got over our first big bust-up Don and I realised that part of the trouble had been living so far apart. He was left with the family in Leeds while I was working in Manchester not able to get home every night. So we moved away from our home town to Chorlton in Manchester to try for a real fresh start. We had a bit of trouble selling the house in Leeds; I don't think the ghost wanted to let us go. But just after the Duckworths got their mortgage we got a bigger mortgage to move across the Pennines.

On screen Vera and Jack had a wonderful house-warming party, with a Spanish theme, using all the tasteful little knick-knacks we had picked up from trips to Benidorm. The Duckworths had this amazing bar fitted out with flashing lights.

Terry was working at the meat market at that time so he brought home loads of sausages that we could have on sticks like they do at posh parties. The only trouble was that Terry didn't bring home the dainty little variety but dirty great big bangers that looked a little strange, to say the least, on the end of cocktail sticks.

Vera had to boot out some gatecrashers, but that was not difficult for her. The main event of the party was in the yard out the back where Fred Gee was trying to prove his athletic abilities as an ex-Paratrooper to our son Terry. Fred jumped off the wall and hurt his back landing on a dustbin. We had a lot of fun doing those scenes.

Just as soon as we had finished the recording we all got on a bus to go to Blackpool where all the cast had been chosen to turn on the lights. So many aspects of my life seem to have turned full circle. My mum always worked in a tailoring factory and I followed her for a time. That was excellent preparation for working in Mike Baldwin's sweatshop! Now Bill Tarmey and I and the rest of the cast were given a marvellous civic reception in Blackpool and handed the honour of switching on the world's greatest illuminations. Doris Speed pulled the big switch in the shape of a Newton & Ridley's beer pump, and I couldn't help thinking back to my days on Woolworth's light bulb counter.

I remember when we went into the Mayor's parlour I felt a little over-awed by the occasion and I decided it was time my behaviour became more refined. I tried to keep really quiet. But then I was introduced to the Lady Mayor, who was a Blackpool landlady, and she had another landlady, one of her friends, as her Mayoress. She just said, 'Hiya kid!' and that was it. All thoughts of refinement went straight out of the window and we were laughing the night away.

We have lots of laughs on *Coronation Street* but in my earlier days all the funny things happened in the factory. They have often involved Lynne Perrie, who plays Ivy, and me. Our careers have followed very similar paths and we have been friends for years. We go back to the club singing days and then we were both in *Leeds United*, although she had a much bigger part than I did. Lynne has never had things easy and we share a lot of attitudes. She has made the transition from cabaret to television quite brilliantly and I really admire her for it.

We were together when we first arrived as workers in the old factory and we have had lots of scenes together. She has this ability to convey enormous emotion. In some of her most harrowing scenes I have seen her cry buckets of tears. For a time I used to nickname her 'Sue Ellen of the Street' after the lady in Dallas who always seemed to be sobbing. She took that in good part.

134

Lynne is a very warm, generous lady. We all felt it very deeply when she was taken ill suddenly, and we were so relieved when she recovered.

We have had lots of fun together over the years. When we made our real-life move over to Chorlton to be nearer the studios we had a big house-warming party. It was a lovely do. The McCann brothers from Liverpool came and provided some impromptu music. One of them just started strumming and they gave us a great turn. A few of the cast came, Anne Kirkbride who plays Deirdre was there, and Lynne came and brought me a lovely cut-glass punch bowl. It was quite a fun do and I quickly filled this punch bowl up and was pouring out drinks like nobody's business with a pan as a ladle.

But I was a bit over-enthusiastic as usual and a crack went right down the side of the bowl. Unfortunately Lynne saw me do it and I tried to cover it up but the bowl was leaking fast where I'd cracked it. I started saying, 'The punch is off.' Lynne came over and said, 'You've cracked it.' I still wouldn't let on and said, 'Where?' She knew though and said, 'I saw you do it.' We finished up having a right laugh about that and in the end we took it back and changed it.

Vera was in trouble a little later for not paying her television licence. She was up in court but when her case was heard she was relieved to be fined £150 instead of the £250 she was expecting. So in Vera's mind she was £100 up. Jack soon solved that problem by getting spectacularly drunk with the money, and he came home and fell, smashing the TV set. So from having had a set with no licence we finished up with a licence and no set. That is the sort of wonderful comic writing which was so invaluable in establishing Jack and Vera.

That first scene where the TV licence inspector knocked at the door and accused me of having a set with no licence will go down in Granada history as one of the longest ever to record. We must have done between twenty and thirty takes for the director that night. I won't name the actor involved because I know he would prefer to forget the whole thing.

He kept knocking on the door and I kept opening it, and from then on the scene was a total disaster. We just couldn't get it right, and the director was very demanding. We went way over the time when the crew went into massive overtime, so it must have cost a fortune in extra payments.

At the end Vinny the prop man asked the actor if he wanted to keep the badge of office he had made up for him. 'You must be joking,' said this actor and he threw the badge angrily on the floor. 'I never want to see it or the Duckworths ever again.' And with that he stormed out.

As if that wasn't bad enough, doing the scene got me and Don talking at home and we suddenly realised we didn't have a licence ourselves, so Don raced straight out and bought one.

Vera was becoming one of those characters who could never have good luck for long. When she won some cash on the bingo that was quickly followed by Jack getting breathalysed and banned from driving. So he managed to lose everything I had gained.

We had some very funny scenes. Jack was trying to settle down to a life of leisure living off the state. To trick the people from the Department of Social Security he hid all our furniture to make it look as though we had been reduced to abject poverty. But an inspector called unexpectedly and caught me and Jack tucking into steak and chips. So we lost out again.

The Duckworths were born to be losers. I got used to that role and although Vera is proud and hard-working I know that she will never be one of life's winners. Even when she pushed Jack into buying Stan Ogden's old window-cleaning round to get him back into being the breadwinner things went wrong. With Terry's help Vera bought the round from Hilda for £100 but when Jack went out he earned just £6 on the first day. The awful truth was that most of Stan's customers had either left the district or died. He was just about as workshy as Jack.

Jack did develop some enthusiasm for his new career when he met up with Dulcie Froggatt, who became the legendary woman from No 21 Inkerman Street. Jack and Dulcie, played by Marji Campi, had an affair. Vera kept feeling sorry for Jack because he was tired. She thought it was from working – she didn't realise it was unpaid overtime put in with Dulcie Froggatt. That was one of so many good stories Jack and

Vera have enjoyed. I laughed when I read it because Jack had amazingly volunteered to work on Boxing Day back in 1984. Vera didn't know but it was just because he thought Dulcie's husband was away working on an oil rig. As it was he came home on holiday unexpectedly so Jack had to clean all the windows in the street to stop him getting suspicious.

A family called the Claytons moved in next door, and Mrs Clayton was a dressmaker. Jack decided they should celebrate their 20th wedding anniversary by going to a cabaret night at the Town Hall, and Connie Clayton worked furiously through the night to get my dress finished.

But it was dreadful. I would have been a laughing stock and I refused to pay the £38.50 bill. Harry Clayton was the milkman and he instantly stopped delivering our milk. This led to me trying to persuade Percy Sugden to change his milkman as the feud developed. It all finished in a big shouting match in the Street. Then our Terry started going out with Andrea Clayton and she got pregnant, so that was more agony for Vera.

Usually it was Jack's escapades that wound Vera up into a rage – like when he was climbing in Dulcie Froggatt's window in Inkerman Street for some extra-curricular activities, fell off a ladder and finished among the garden gnomes. That was a marvellous scene, and you know Jack always tries to come up smelling of roses. Even though he finished up in hospital that time he bounced back by chatting up the nurses. I think that is

GRANADA TELEVISION
Manchester M60 9EA
Telephone 061-832 7211
36 Golden Square, London W1R 4AH
Telephone 01-734 8080

CORONATION STREET
Monday, May 23, 1983, 7.30pm.

Vera Duckworth now knows that her husband Jack has been passing himself off at
the video-dating agency as the unmarried "Vince St Clair." And, with Bet
Lynch's help, she plans to get her revenge in Granada's CORONATION STREET on
Monday, May 23 at 7.30pm.

ELIZABETH DAWN and WILLIAM TARMEY are the Duckworths and JULIE GOODYEAR plays
Bet Lynch.   P694/2310

SXG/LD/DJH/050583/100

COPYRIGHT GRANADA.   REPRODUCTION FREE FOR USE AS PROGRAMME PUBLICITY ONLY.

Top: Vera suspects Jack of
becoming 'Vince st Clair' the star
of the video dating agency while
Bet Lynch looks on.

Right: Dustin Gee and Liz Dawn as
they really looked, without
their wigs.

I told Prince Charles he was my favourite Royal but he said: "It won't get you anywhere."

Top: Duncan Walker is one of the world's real stars. I so admire his work at Killingbeck Hospital.

Above: The dynamic Duckworths, Jack and Vera and son Terry.

Dustin Hoffman was taking a close look at my wig. He had just finished wearing one in 'Tootsie' so I think it was professional interest.

Top: I pushed my grandson on an eight mile charity walk.

Above right: Coronation Street is very popular in Canada. Bill Tarmey and I were treated like Royalty.

Above left: I dance with Wayne Sleep, the man who danced with the Princess of Wales.

Above: Two big comics in every sense. The late great Les Dawson and
Paul Shane.

Opposite: Jack and Vera.

A Caribbean cruise was a holiday of a lifetime for
Don and I.

why Jack and Vera make such a good partnership. They battle away like deadly enemies yet deep down underneath I think they have a happy marriage.

I was really getting to know Vera by now and I was always keen to ensure that she was more than just a big mouth. I think her heart's bigger than her mouth anyway. Once my dentist was reaching in to do some painful work on my teeth that required me to open really wide. Afterwards I told him he was the only man who could say he had put his hand in the biggest mouth in the land. He still laughs about that to this day.

Besides, it is not all gloom and doom for Vera. In 1986 she won a car in a magazine competition all because Jack filled in a coupon in her name suggesting himself as Husband of the Year. Jack came up with the slogan for Vera to say: 'My husband deserves to be Husband of the Year because since the day we married he has made my life one long holiday.' Jack thought he would take the car, but I was delighted when Vera had other ideas.

He reached out for the keys but I refused to let him have them. Vera had driving lessons and in spite of Jack's derision she proved to be a natural and passed her driving test with flying colours at the first attempt on 9 July 1986. In my first run behind the wheel I chauffeured Ivy and Shirley Armitage, played by Lisa Lewis, out on a run to a night club.

Unfortunately Ivy got a bit tipsy and finished up coming home with some sequinned pants worn by the male stripper. Unknown to Vera, Jack had had some duplicate keys cut and when he sneakily borrowed the car for a late-night passion session with Dulcie Froggatt he discovered these incriminating underpants under the seat. But Jack couldn't confront Vera with what he was convinced was evidence of her infidelity because he was not supposed to have driven the car. Eventually the truth came out in its usual hilarious way.

Soon after that we had the great fire of Coronation Street, which was really Jack's fault. He got fed up with having to dash down the cellar to replace the fuse when the lights in the Rovers Return kept going out. So he put in a 30 amp fuse that was much too big instead of getting the real electrical problem seen to.

When I passed my test in real life it was like something out of a comedy script. Amazingly I drove so well in my automatic car that the examiner passed me for manual as well! He had to come round later and say he had overstretched himself.

But when I was younger and tried to drive I was a total disaster. Once I had a lesson booked and forgot about it. When I got home Don said, 'Your instructor has been waiting for ten minutes.'

I jumped in the car and I must have been driving for about five minutes when he said, 'Oh, you're doing ever so well. I can't believe it's the same person.'

I said, 'Well, I did have a couple of brandies on the way home to steady my nerves.' He yelled, 'Stop the car.' I was far from an ideal pupil. Another time he said that I was driving so fast that if I passed my test I would get done for speeding.

In the end the instructor's wife told me that he had been taking people out since he was in the Army and never before had he woken her up in the night screaming 'Clutch!' at the top of his voice.

So after being written off as a motorist I abandoned any real plans I had to learn to drive. I was always a bad passenger. Don used to drive fast when we were going to a club for one of my singing appearances. If we had had a row he would drive even faster.

It was not until years later that a funny thing happened. I was forty-nine years old and going through one of my down periods. It was when Don was buying and selling cars and I felt really bad and just said to him, 'Don, get me in that car over there. I want to drive.'

He said, 'Don't be silly, you can't drive.' But I insisted and got into this car and somehow I thought that just turning the ignition on would calm my nerves. I started it up and drove all over this waste ground with Don looking at me open-mouthed, and the remarkable thing was that it did calm my nerves.

It was an old Austin Princess, an automatic, worth about £2,000 I think. I said to Don, 'I want this car. I am going to learn to drive at last.' I got L-plates and my cleaner Pat took me out driving in it. When I came to take my test in Bury, I put my hand-brake on at every light and really concentrated, and I passed first time.

I found that with concentrating on driving and

building up confidence as I went along, my nerves never bothered me once. Gradually I felt more and more relaxed. I never did have time to have that nervous breakdown.

10
Storms at Home

Anybody looking at me would think I had a wonderful life. I have fame and fortune and all the things that go with it. I have a good job, a nice house with a new car in the drive, but most important of all I have a marvellous family.

I was lucky to have fine healthy children who are giving me fine healthy grandchildren to love and cherish.

I know in my heart that God has been watching over me and that I have been very, very fortunate. But there has been a price. I came from anything but a show business background so I had no real preparation for any of the things I've done.

I had a good voice at school so I found myself singing in clubs, which was something altogether different. I only had a vague idea how to play a part, and I found myself an actress. I could wind myself up to look confident on the outside, but inside I would be as steady as a jellyfish on a motorbike.

Everyone thinks how lucky I've been, and I can't deny that. I have always had this amazing knack of being in the right place at the right time. But from where I'm looking at it my life has been a battle, in my career and in my marriage.

I owe everything I have to *Coronation Street*. It has given me everything, but there have still been times when I feel I have given it everything as well.

Don and I were never one of your lovey-dovey couples. We're more like a couple of warriors, who need each other to keep the battle going. We both have strong personalities and we have always argued. There was a time when I was petrified about what the neighbours might think. If Don and I had a row the worst thing he could do would be to open all the windows and bellow out, 'I don't care what the neighbours think.'

I often sit and think I would have been much happier if Don had stayed an electrician and I had been content to sit at home and do my ironing and be a happy housewife. I'm no raving feminist, me. I often think I would have been delighted to have been a kept woman. But it just didn't turn out like that. I wanted a bit extra for my kids. I didn't just want enough to eat and somewhere to live, I wanted enough to go on holiday and have nice clothes for them all as well.

We had only ever been to Scarborough and Bridlington and places like that, but when we first went on holiday abroad I put my foot in it in a big way. We were in a fish restaurant on the beach near Torremolinos in Spain and we were serenaded by this chap playing a mandolin.

It was really romantic, with palm trees and the sun setting over the Mediterranean. He came and sang to me and then held out an ashtray. Without thinking I tapped the ash off my cigarette into it.

As soon as I did it I knew I'd made a big mistake. He was hoping for money, not cigarette ash. I was so embarrassed I cleaned it out with my dress.

The funniest row Don and I ever had was years ago, driving down York Road in Leeds. We had had a bit of a difference beforehand and I'd been in the shop getting a wig fitted for about an hour. It was all lacquered and stuck up. As soon as I got into the car we started arguing again.

He flipped and grabbed my new wig and threw it straight out of the window of the car. It rolled down the road like a furry football gathering dust, litter and tab-ends as it went. It upset me at the time, but now we always laugh at it.

Another time after I had been singing we had a ding-dong of a row in a motorway café. He said, 'I'm going home. You can make your own way home.' We were yelling at each other and two chaps came up and one of them said, 'Is this man bothering you?'

I said, 'Yes.' Don said, 'I'm her husband.' But I just said, 'I've never set eyes on him before in my life,' and they ushered him out. I did feel a little bit guilty, but this other club act who knew us both went and brought Don back in.

Fate intervenes in some extraordinary ways. Doors open and close for people at different times for different things. I know they have for me.

We had Graham from the start, Don and I, and then Dawn came along quickly and the other two followed.

We could all have lived quite happily on an electrician's pay all right but I wanted more. And then along came my chance at *Coronation Street*.

Coronation Street is a fantastic programme. I am really proud to be in the best television programme in Britain. It's a privilege to go to work there where the standards are so high, but it's not easy.

I felt the pressure building up from the start. In the early days you go in and you're in danger of being over-awed by the whole experience. It is like a vast efficient machine and you are on edge to make sure your little cog in the great wheel never goes wrong.

Then when Vera became established I was not given a regular's contract. I never knew if the next stint would be my last. So I had to keep up my singing in the clubs. And of course when a club got a *Coronation Street* character doing a turn, that used to pack in the punters and my money grew and grew.

But the demands of the two jobs grew and grew as well. I would be racing all over the country to fulfil my commitments. I think the real strain on our marriage began then.

Don was great in the early days particularly. He would take time off work so I could have a sleep in the afternoons before a singing engagement. He looked after the kids a lot more than most men in those days. He would happily feed them and change the nappies while I was getting my songs ready for the night.

But as it all grew he gradually had to take so much

time off that he became a full-time manager. He had to. It made perfect sense from a financial point of view. I was earning more and I needed somebody I could rely on, and who can you trust better than your husband?

On the other hand, that does not make for an easy relationship. Don is a proud man. Just because it made sense from a practical and business point of view did not mean it made it easy for Don to accept that he was really working for me.

We had always had a fairly volatile relationship, but just as Vera was starting to really register with the viewers as a popular character there were some even more difficult times ahead. I would get home from work really drained and tired, and Don would be wanting to talk about bookings and engagements. I sometimes simply couldn't face it and told him so in my usual direct way. It made his job difficult, and he found that frustrating.

It was a difficult situation for both of us. In a way I resented it because I was snowed under with work which I have always found very demanding. Learning lines has never come easily to me.

Having a husband as your professional manager can create a tense relationship. Work tends to take over every part of your home life, and I'm not sure that is a good thing. It certainly wasn't for us, anyway.

I won't go into all the details of our problems. Some things that happened are too private and painful to recall, for Don and myself and for the children. The thing about being in *Coronation Street* is that you can't have a new hairdo without making headline news. There is a lot of pressure, and it is relentless. It never lets up. I had never really been prepared for that. The Press interest is simply phenomenal. I can't begin to tell you what a goldfish bowl sort of life that makes for us.

Recently I went on a cruise in the Caribbean. It was idyllic, a real getting-away-from-it-all break. But there was a woman on the cruise whose suitcase went missing. She was without a lot of her clothes and, as we were roughly the same size, I offered to lend her some of mine.

That trivial little event ended up splashed all over every newspaper in Britain. Don't get me wrong, I don't mind the papers taking an interest and I know it's only because so many *Street* viewers are fascinated by everything we do.

That was innocent, but when your face gets famous you find there are lots of 'users' who appear in your life. I mean people who want to somehow use the popularity of your character and the programme. The newspapers are always there, of course, but there are other people who are more subtle in their ways of using. You find you are invited to open or endorse or visit all manner of things.

Very often the request is straightforward and helps a good cause. Then I am only too keen to use whatever so-called celebrity status the *Street* has given me. But being fairly open and straightforward myself sometimes I find myself involved with people I don't like.

Becoming famous puts a lot of responsibility on your shoulders, and you have to learn how to handle it. When I was younger and less experienced I was naive and I did get myself in situations I would have been well advised to steer clear of.

The first big wave of publicity is the one that always knocks you sideways, and if it looks as though you have a new man in your life you become a sensation that pushes important world events off the front pages. Most of the things that were written about Don and me during our darker days of parting and getting back together again were a lot of nonsense. Half a fact was frequently dressed up with plenty of imagination to make a story.

The full details are for Don and me to know. But because I want this book to be as straight and as honest as people who have parted with hard-earned brass deserve, I will try to give you a flavour of the more diffi-cult moments of a *Coronation Street* marriage.

I did have an affair. It was a long time ago. It started out as nothing more than a discreet friendship, but it fin-ished up as headline news in all the newspapers. Of course I regret what happened and the hurt it caused to many people. It affected them deeply. My family are everything to me. Their love is my greatest strength.

At this time I had a lot of unhappiness inside me and sometimes I tried to find the answer to my problems in a bottle. There are thousands of people who can tell you that drinking is no answer to anything. But they all had to find out for themselves. At the time a drink or two simply seems to ease the pain and help you get through the day.

I don't believe it affected my work. It was usually after a busy day when I preferred to have a drink to help me forget my problems.

I never drank very much when I was young. I started drinking, sometimes heavily, the day after that doctor told me how ill my mother was. After that I slipped into drinking in the house. And it became serious drinking, not just drinking for pleasure when I was out socially like I had done before, but drinking to blot out the pressure.

At first it was just a pick-me-up, something to give me a quick boost when I was feeling down. Then it was a refuge from unhappiness, from the stress of the job, from life. Actors are noted for drinking and I suppose I shouldn't be surprised. It's a pressure job.

Don and I were becoming like the couple in the film *The Wars of the Roses*. I think if we hadn't split up at times we would have ended up killing each other. At our worst that's how bad it became. I don't think anyone lived like we did. Our feelings ran high as we struggled to come to terms with everything.

At times it felt as if the world was closing in on me. To outsiders I was bold and brassy Vera who would never let a simple thing like a man get in the way of anything. I always had to look smart, seem confident and happy. But inside often I was churning with emotion.

So Don and I did spend some times apart. Often it was not a big, dramatic split up, but just a night or two's breathing space from each other.

It really knocked me for six when my dad was taken seriously ill with lung cancer. It was awful. When my mother was poorly I had been the main one to look after her, but with my dad I was working in Manchester on the wrong side of the Pennines from Leeds so the regular routine tasks of caring were taken up by my brother Albert and his family. But I was determined to do what I could. When I had a break from the *Street* I said, 'Right, Dad, I'm going to take you to the sunshine.'

I booked for us all to go to Spain, to Torremolinos – me and Don and my dad. It was something new for my dad. He was very down to earth and not at all an experienced traveller. Just after we had taken off from Manchester we were having a very welcome cuppa with our meal when he turned to me and said, 'This tea is off.'

I said, 'It can't be off.' When I called the stewardess over to investigate I discovered he had mistaken those little packets they give you with airline meals, and my poor dad had put salt into his tea.

When we got to the hotel, I said, 'Right, I'll unpack. You go down and have a sit in the sun.' I went up to the room and sorted the suitcases out. When I went down to the pool I couldn't believe it. My dad was sitting back on a sun lounger, in his vest, with a handkerchief on his head knotted at the four corners of course. He still had his trousers, shoes and socks on.

Don said, 'Look at your dad. We can't leave him there like that.' I said, 'You shut up. If my dad's happy then he can lie down how he likes.'

Then a bus full of women from England arrived and inevitably they all seemed to be *Coronation Street* fans. 'Vera!' they shouted together and came rushing over. 'What are you doing here?' I explained that I was there with Don and my father. Well, they made such an excited fuss of my dad he couldn't believe it.

'Albert,' they started shouting. 'How are you?' And they all crowded round. My dad couldn't be bothered with their questions, and after a while he said firmly to me, 'Will you tell these women to leave me alone. I can't be doing with them.'

He had never been abroad before. There were quite a few Germans staying in this hotel. My dad was at the bar when all his worst suspicions of foreigners in general and Germans in particular were confirmed when this big German purposely stood on his foot to push in front of him at the bar. He was really annoyed.

A few days later we were sitting in one of the lounges and my dad said he was going outside. I warned him it wasn't as warm as it looked. As we went onto the patio I pulled the curtains back from a big glass door closed to shield him from the breeze.

Just after we settled down a big German marched straight into the glass and really hurt himself. The curtain had been partly a safety thing to stop people walking into the window, which can be dangerous.

This German was all right though, he just bounced off. But it did look like something out of Laurel and Hardy. I had been faffing around for my dad to make it comfortable for him and I hadn't thought about that. The German was still rubbing his head when I and my dad walked quickly away trying to stop from giggling. My dad said, 'That's the one who stood on my foot.' So he got his just deserts. My dad and I did laugh. Well, we are from Yorkshire.

He still went out when he was ill. Right to the end he was his good-natured self. I have so many happy memories of him. He had some very funny ways. He never quite got used to his false teeth. He always had two hankies, one for his teeth and one for his nose. When he came in the house he would take his teeth out and he would often leave them. Many's the time we've all laughed because he would be halfway up the road to the club and I'd be shouting out of the door, 'Dad, you've forgotten your teeth.'

He was so proud at me being in the show and I was so pleased to be able to help him in his last years. We had moved over to Chorlton by then so it was harder for me to see him as often as I wanted. I was worried sick about him and it was hard to concentrate on doing lines. I got myself into quite a state.

I would keep rushing out of work and racing over there, but Maisie told me not to. She said, 'Look, I can go every day because I'm nearer. You come when you can. You did it for my mother.'

The worst moment came at the end. I had been to visit him the night before he died and my dad had really gone downhill. When I got home I was very upset. I said to Don, 'He's not right, my dad.' Don said, 'Don't worry. They would tell you if there was something really wrong with him.'

But the next morning I rang my brother Albert to find out how dad was. But Albert wasn't there, he'd already gone over to the hospital, so instantly I feared the worst. I just jumped in a taxi and raced over there.

I dashed back to Killingbeck Hospital and went in through some French windows. Everybody else was waiting for me at the other side of the ward, where I should have gone.

I got to his bed and it had screens all round it. I didn't think, I just pulled a screen back and there he was, lying there, dead. My legs buckled. After that I was in a daze. I felt like I had hurled myself out of an aeroplane without a parachute. I have often felt that after that minute I was launched firmly on the dangerous path to self-destruction.

He had been in and out of hospital for a time. I am just glad that he did not linger on in hospital and suffer terribly. That at least was a small mercy.

If I had one wish it would be to see a cure for all cancers in my lifetime. I know there have been a lot of improvements in the treatment and a lot of people have recovered, but I just hope for a really reliable cure. Wouldn't that be wonderful?

The stress that led to all the problems in my life stemmed a lot from my parents going. I was so fond of them and I still miss them both very badly. After my dad died my life went to pieces in many ways. The job and my marriage seemed to throw up more problems than I knew what to do with. I found myself acting, even when I had stopped being Vera. But I was in a real depression, and the difficulties at home get worse and worse.

When the newspaper headlines broadcast the details of my affair I thought I was going to die. It was terrible. The headline was, 'I pined for my lover.' It went on and on. It was a load of rubbish but it re-opened a lot of old but still very tender wounds and caused endless anguish to me both privately and professionally.

It was so horrific that it put my father's death out of my mind, and I will always feel that the awful press coverage stopped me from grieving for my father properly.

Can you imagine my horror when at the very moment of leaving on a family holiday those ghastly headlines appeared about me and my private life. Private life? That's a laugh. I had just about the most public private life possible. Everyone could read the lurid detail in the newspapers. Every time a newspaper rustled I would cringe with embarrassment. There was an awful picture of me with my legs up in the air with a feather boa.

I didn't recognise the woman in the story as me. It was like a ghastly nightmare. The story outside had nothing to do with the real truth inside. I felt powerless and alone. I wanted to hide somewhere safe, but I felt I had nowhere to turn.

Don and I had split up before this. But in the summer of 1984 we split up again in the most painful and public way possible. I moved out to a flat in Salford. It was the worst period of my life.

This time we hired solicitors to help us do battle with each other, and that was perhaps the most expensive mistake we ever made. We ended up paying out thousands of pounds to land ourselves with more anguish and more dreadful publicity.

It is at times like that when you find out who your real friends are. Jack Diamond lived up to his name many times over. Jack is a colourful club character from Blackpool, and when my flat became besieged by press men he provided me with a bolthole by the seaside.

Don and 1 were arguing, through our solicitors, over household possessions. I remember he insisted that I couldn't take some false eyelashes because they were not on the agreed list! This is the sort of situation you get in when you fight your battles through lawyers. At the time I had very few possessions with me because they were all in my house, and Don was holding the fort.

Once I rang him up and screamed that I simply couldn't take any more and that I was going to commit suicide, and he came rushing round to my little place.

When he arrived, he walked up and rang the bell and I opened the door and threw a full bucket of water all over him. He was soaked wet through but I think the shock of it made him laugh because he was half wondering if I would still be alive when he arrived.

I was in such a state then that I used to ring up all the time and he would ring me and we took to arguing over the phone. I would say, 'Are you in that bed that I paid for?' 'Are you using that phone that is mine?' – awful things like that, because I was stuck in the tiny place and I didn't have anything.

Once when we'd had a row over the phone he came round to the house I was living in and pulled the telephone wires from the outside. I was inside being dragged across the room. It was like a farce, really, except we weren't laughing at the time.

I woke up the morning after the court case and it was one of the worst days of my life. I sent a friend to Victoria Station in Manchester to buy all the papers and I got them and spread them all over my bed. I couldn't believe the headlines.

I stayed in a hotel bedroom in Blackpool for a week, and you know what it's like at the seaside in the summer, I could see lots of people out with buckets and spades and I'd think I would give anything to be one of them.

Jack Diamond used to bring me in a tray and look after me. He was wonderful, and now we still laugh about it because I used to write on one of my hand-out photos, 'Thank you, Nurse Diamond. The patient is feeling a little better today.' He's still got them. You need a friend at times like that. That was one of my lowest points.

Gradually some common sense came into the situation and Don and I began to talk again. Eventually we got back together and slowly put back the pieces of our marriage. In the years since I have tried to make sense of it all.

So I picked my life up and decided I was not going to look backwards, I was going to go forward. There were still some battles ahead.

One night after a row developed in a restaurant Don took me home and put me to bed. But they rang up from the restaurant and seemed a bit disappointed that our differences had become so heated we had forgotten to pay the bill.

Don went back to pay, thinking I was asleep, but I was still awake and I was lying there fuming. When he went out I got up and grabbed all his clothes out of the wardrobe and started cutting them up. I hacked all his trousers apart at the seams, then I bundled all his suits up in my arms and carried them round to the back of the house and stuffed them in the dustbin.

I wasn't thinking straight, thanks to drinking too much, but I was just so angry at Don I was determined to do anything I could to get back at him.

Anyone who has allowed themselves to have one or two drinks too many will know that what seems to be a 100 per cent great idea last thing at night is often a disaster when you wake up the next day.

In the morning I opened the wardrobe door and a trouser leg dropped down. I thought, 'My God. What have I done?' I rang wardrobe at Granada and said, 'I've had an accident with these suits.'

I got into a taxi, hidden (I hoped) by dark glasses and a headscarf, with the biggest suitcase you have ever seen. I arrived at a wonderful repairers who can work miracles with costumes. I opened the case and tipped this big pile on the counter.

The man said, 'What's happened?' I said, 'Well, I've had a bit of an accident.' He did his best, poor chap, but those clothes were never really quite the same.

That crazy night became quite a sobering experience for me. I was really frightened by what I had done while under the influence of alcohol. When I spoke to Don later I said, 'I'm not going to drink any more.' I am not sure whether he believed me or not, but I didn't have another alcoholic drink for five years. It scared me that much. I have only been a social drinker ever since.

This period of my life had whirled me along on some kind of crazy fun fair ride. I never really had time to reflect on what was going on. But when I seemed to be at my very lowest point God gave me the strength and the belief to rebuild my life and my faith in myself. Looking back now, I realise that I was not in control. Perhaps we all feel guilty at times for different reasons. I know now that I was punishing and hurting myself because I felt a lack of self-worth. I didn't believe I really mattered as a person. Somewhere along the way the real me had got lost.

I would say to anyone facing what seems to be overwhelming problems, start believing in yourself and take one day and one step at a time. The human spirit is a wonderful thing. It's easy to look at other people and think they never have any problems and that you have all the bad luck. What I have learned is to thank God for the many good things I have achieved. I realise now how very lucky I am to have stardom and success but more importantly to have my wonderful children and their unconditional love. I also like myself and know now that I do deserve to be happy. From this dark period of my life I have found light and the ability to see what really matters in this world.

11
Working for Charity

I never thought I had deserved to be special. I had lacked confidence in myself, though you might not have guessed it. Perhaps that was my best acting achievement.

It's a funny experience having complete strangers crowd round you for your autograph. There is no training for it and everyone handles it in different ways. Who knows exactly what sort of effects it has on you, being the focus of that much attention? Because of my own personal sorrows I have gained much more understanding of other people's.

Of course, as a character in *Coronation Street* you are not a complete stranger to the *Street's* fans. You are like a close friend to most of them. After all, you do blast into their living rooms three times a week, so from their point of view you're practically a member of the family. I have been honoured by the real affection and kindness I have received from many, many fans.

I think I have got used to the attention now, but it takes some adjusting to. One of the things I noticed quite early on in my times of meeting fans was that it's usually the fittest and boldest who push to the front.

Inevitably this means that the less able and the less

confident people tend to get pushed to the back of the queue. I gradually realised there was a small but constant presence of deaf people among the viewers coming to meet me. They always seemed to stand politely aside and hopefully wait their turn, which sometimes, due to the sheer numbers, did not come.

I decided that it would be good to learn sign language so that I could communicate properly with deaf people. After all, you could even do that from the other side of the room!

That was what decided me to take an interest in Hennessey House, a residential home for the deaf in Manchester. But first of all I had a word with a priest, at the church over the road from where we live in Manchester. He suggested I went to St Joseph's Church for the Deaf. I went along to a Mass with Pat, a friend, and just sat at the back.

The whole thing was really moving, with the priest saying things in sign language. I was overcome with emotion. There was a nun playing a guitar and they had a deaf choir. You have to smile at the idea but I wasn't laughing that day, it was really touching. They were from Hennessey House, and there I met Father O'Mara.

He is a very good-looking, charismatic priest, a wonderful man. He told me that what they really needed was a new coach for outings. The one they had was falling to bits.

So I said, 'What is more important in your eyes, me learning sign language or me trying to raise some money?' He smiled, looked at me and said, 'Well, we could do with the money.' He enthused me and I threw myself into organising charity events for him.

We organised a big concert to get the ball rolling at Old Trafford. I got a lot of help from friends. Lynne Perrie did a spot, dear old Bill Tarmey sang and I got a lot of club acts to come along as well. We raised £8,000 in one night. Then we organised another charity walk and raised enough for eight phonic ears to help deaf children at a school for deaf youngsters that only had two phonic ears that they had to share round before then.

The walk turned out to be a wonderful fund-raiser. We got companies to sponsor different walkers and I called on a lot of my *Coronation Street* colleagues. We got everyone kitted out in white T-shirts for our eight-mile walk. Michael le Vell was the one who attracted the most company sponsorship, and that was a great success.

I love to use the power of *Coronation Street* to do a bit of good if I can. When I appeared on *Wogan* I wore a T-shirt promoting the Booth Hall Hospital appeal. I was quite shy at first and kept my jacket over it, but by the end of the show I was displaying the message about this special event as best I could. It certainly worked – nearly 200,000 people turned up.

The phone never stops ringing. I do a lot of charity work. I always have. I started long before I was famous. But when other hard-working people have raised some money for a good cause and then I go along and present a cheque, I always say, 'I feel a fraud.' If I can bring a bit of limelight to an occasion and help, then I'm delighted, but there are so many unsung heroes and heroines behind the scenes in the charity world that nobody ever seems to find out about.

But I genuinely get pleasure from giving. Many, many times I have made a contribution or some appearance for a charity, and the very next week something really nice has happened for me.

Coronation Street has given me the confidence to do things I never would have thought I'd achieve. Bill Tarmey and I were asked down to appear on the BBC's *Children in Need* show. It was a very good cause and we were pleased to do it.

They sent a tape up for me and Bill to sing the song, 'Yes, I Remember It Well', that everyone remembers Maurice Chevalier singing. Going down on the train I said to Bill, 'We are going to look right idiots because I can't remember the song and we are supposed to sit on this park bench set they have got looking smart and sophisticated, would you believe, and do the song properly.'

I knew there were going to be stars from West End musicals in the line-up with polished performances of very well rehearsed shows that we could never compete with. So we decided to stay firmly in character. I said, 'Look, Bill, you've brought your pyjamas and I've got my nightie,' because we were staying overnight. 'Why don't we do a Duckworths scene? Let's forget the park bench and have a simple breakfast scene. We only need a table, a bottle of milk, a 2 lb bag of sugar and so on.' I said, 'We're not singing properly, we're doing a Duck-worth.' And he agreed, bless him.

When it came to the performance I took my lead from Bill because he is very good musically and it went brilliantly, even if I do say so myself. I had the lines on my mirror and he had his hidden in the sugar bowl, and it was a right laugh. We weren't overshadowed at all.

One of the best events I've been involved with was a fund-raising weekend on the *Krypton Factor* assault course near Bury for Booth Hall Hospital. We raised over £200,000 with having teams sponsored, and a per-centage went to the Army Benevolent fund. Amounts of money like that can do a tremendous amount of good.

When people see Vera looming up, it certainly opens doors. I love to get involved. Don and I once went to a jumble sale at a big BUPA hospital and there was a stall with all these really nice curtains they were getting rid of. I got straight on the phone to St Joseph's, bought all the curtains and took them straight round and helped the nuns to put them up. They looked smashing. There's nothing like a bit of direct action.

We went to a disco at St Joseph's once. Deaf peo-ple might not hear the music, but they receive the vibrations through the air. The only trouble was when Don went to the bar he couldn't get a drink because they couldn't hear him and he didn't do sign language. Bill Tarmey and his wife were with us and they thought that was a huge joke.

I danced with Wayne Sleep just after he had danced with the Princess of Wales. I said to him, 'Come on. You danced with Diana, now dance with me.' I just wanted to be able to say I danced with the man who danced with the woman who married the Prince of Wales. He was very nice, even if he did only come up to my chin. It was at the *Say No To Drugs* event at the Adelphi Theatre in London. That was an amazing experience for me because I opened the show. There were some dancers on and then it was up to me to get things going. I was petrified because I hardly had time to rehearse. I couldn't get over the fact that Sacha Distel was on the bill, I've always liked him so much.

Neil Kinnock was there, playing himself in a sketch with Faith Brown as Margaret Thatcher. That was really funny, and afterwards I got talking to him and telling him about my little sister Maisie being a Labour councillor. He was brilliant. We all ended up back at Stringfellows afterwards. That delighted my sister.

The great thing about doing charity work is that it brings you into contact with people from totally different fields. Sometimes I feel embarrassed that I have this strange thing called fame which always brings in such enthusiastic support and people who do wonderful, important work go unnoticed.

One of the many people I've got to know is a surgeon at Killingbeck Hospital called Duncan Walker. With an earring in one ear he looks nothing like one of the best doctors in England, but just being on the fringes of the lives of people like him enriches my own life more than I can ever say.

Sometimes I surprise myself and come out with remarks that are pure Vera. I went to a party at Frank Lamar's – he is a real character who is also known as Fufu or Mr Manchester. He's another marvellous bloke who does so much for charity. We were enjoying the evening with a few drinks when he introduced me to a man called Harold Riley. I didn't know he was a famous artist, I'm afraid, and when I asked what he did Frank said, 'Oh he paints. He has just painted the Opera House.'

I said, 'What? On his own?' – thinking in all ignorance that he was a painter and decorator. It just seemed like an enormous job for one man. Everyone fell about laughing, including Harold Riley I'm happy to say. He certainly saw the funny side.

Another time my mouth sprang into action without fully engaging my brain was when Bill Tarmey and I appeared on a special charity edition of the television quiz show *3–2–1*. Nina Myscow was there playing a witch in one of the sketches. She had such long false fingernails that she was worried about how on earth she was going to be able to go to the loo. I kindly offered to pull her knickers down!

Jack and Vera were pitched against two other soap opera couples for the main contest with Ted Rodgers in his usual role as host. In the first round we had to finish off geographical phrases and our question was

'Khyber?'. Bill straight away said 'Pass' but I screamed, 'No, no. Don't pass. I might know it!' The audience went crazy with laughter at that.

Then the next question was, 'What is a chippie?' I piped up, 'It's a chip shop,' and the audience burst into floods of laughter again. We got knocked out and the couples from *Brookside* and *Emmerdale* went on to compete in the final. I don't think I've got a big future as a quiz show contestant.

Vera's mailbag at Granada is always brimming over. Many letters are absolutely heart-breaking. Some people seem to be struck by the most appalling strings of bad luck. There's not a lot that I can do in most cases, but if a signed photograph helps to ease anybody's pain then I'm happy to oblige.

I don't ever want to lose touch with ordinary people. If I do that I'll have grown too big for my boots. The other day, for instance, I got this letter from a lady in Manchester. I had been away from the *Street* on a rare six-week break, and this was waiting for me:

> Dear Liz,
>
> I don't know if you remember me but I spoke to you one night about fifteen months ago in a club in Manchester. I explained to you that I had just started raising money for breast cancer at Withington and Christie's Hospital. It was very noisy in the club that night and you asked me to write to you to tell you what I wanted.

I lost my mother when I was just six years old. She died of breast cancer at the age of forty-one after fighting the disease for four years. Although some doctors say that this cancer is not hereditary I had my first breast removed at the age of thirty-seven. I had my second one removed a year later.

Fortunately for me, thanks to all the research I have a far better chance of survival than my poor mother. Once I passed my forty-first birthday I felt that it was time to look ahead and try to get on with my life. I worry for my daughter, who is twenty-three. I hope and pray that she does not have to go through the same ordeal. The doctors reckon that by the time she is my age there will be even more amazing medical developments and there will be some sort of prevention available if not a complete cure.

I am deluged by letters, but how can you not try to offer some help when they are like that? You see I know that *Coronation Street* goes right into people's hearts as well as their homes. A lot of them really love Vera Duckworth, loud as she is. Whatever it is that they have written about, it is important to them.

In fact because that letter had been waiting for a few weeks I rang the sender up. The lady said, 'I can't believe you're actually telephoning me at home.' I said, 'Well, why not?'

I find it impossible not to be touched by real people. A woman stopped when I was rushing through Kendal's on one of my lunchtime shopping expeditions. She told me such a tale of heartbreak I found myself spending my whole lunch break with her. But I didn't mind. If I can use a bit of Vera to make someone forget their problems for a minute or two, then I think it's well worth it.

Once I was a guest at an old people's home in Yorkshire and they showed me round to meet all the residents. It was an open day and the place looked lovely. One old dear was past watching anything on television, even *Coronation Street*. She hadn't a clue who I was, and when the nurse told her I was Vera Duckworth she didn't quite hear properly and got into her head I was Vera Lynn, one of her all-time favourite stars, apparently.

Her face lit up and she said, 'Ooh, Vera Lynn.' The nurse started to try to say, 'No, it's Vera Duckworth,' but I hushed her up and sang two verses of 'There'll Be Blue Birds Over the White Cliffs of Dover'. It made that old dear's day. I don't suppose Vera Lynn would have minded.

12
Twenty Years on the Street

It's hard work on *Coronation Street*, but don't let anyone tell you we don't find the odd bit of time to have
some fun.

There are a number of practical jokers among the
cast who see it as part of their role in life to amuse the
rest of us. Sometimes it works brilliantly, but sometimes
it doesn't.

Phil Middlemiss made me laugh because after the
funeral for his character Des's girlfriend Lisa he said he
fancied having the brass plate off her coffin. Someone
unscrewed it and gave it to him. He's got it in his dressing room. Now isn't that morbid?

My heart sank when I got the script about Vera res-
cuing a cat in Baldwin's factory because as you know I
have always been terrified of cats. The first scene wasn't
so bad because it was just getting an empty box – we
didn't have to have the cat inside.

But then I had to take it into the factory and let it out
of the box. While I was waiting for the scene to start this
cat was going mental, jumping up and down in the box. I
shouted to the floor manager but he just said, 'Don't
worry, you'll be all right.'

I had to go into the factory and say, 'Here she is –

Cleo.' Well, it certainly wasn't a Cleo, it was a Tom. I just shut my eyes and went for it. I put my hand in and lifted it out. But the poor creature was frightened to death, and it just weed over everything. It was awful. They said, 'Right, that's it for today. We'll pick it up tomorrow.' I never slept that night thinking about how things could get worse.

Vera has had some wonderful scenes over the years, often with her bungling husband Jack. I think my messiest moment came when Jack had to unblock our chimney. He was doing the job himself to save money as usual and it had to end with a huge fall of soot covering him, me and our front room.

Not surprisingly, they left the scene until last that day, and when Bill did it he seemed to drag down more soot than anyone could have imagined. It covered both of us and went everywhere. The director was delighted and the scene was very funny. But my problem was that I was due to present a cheque at a bingo hall in Sheffield not long afterwards. And I really didn't want to turn up looking like a one-woman revival of the *Black and White Minstrels*.

Soot was up my nose, in my ears and all down my neck. The make-up girl did help me to get washed a bit but when I dashed on stage I still had bits of soot in my hair and all down my neck. I hope the people of Sheffield weren't too alarmed by my grubby appearance. I felt a real mess and no mistake.

My most anxious moments come when I have to

get behind the wheel of the Vauxhall Nova that I won in the contest. It's a manual gearbox and I can still only manage an automatic. So usually there are a load of men at the back, carefully out of shot, pushing the car when you see Vera at the wheel.

I was taking Ivy out for a drive somewhere and they were filming us leaving Coronation Street. The only trouble was I didn't even have the ignition on so the steering lock was still making the car turn. These six blokes pushed away and I screamed but they didn't stop and we swerved straight across the Street into the sound recordist's van and knocked his door off. That was a real laugh.

Driving has never been my strong point. When I first won the car there used to be a stunt double, complete with her own curly wig, to stand in and actually drive the car for me. But when there was a story where the factory girls had to motor off in search of Mike Baldwin this woman was nowhere to be seen.

I pleaded with the director that I couldn't handle a car with a manual gearbox, especially with four of us in the car, but he said, 'It's all right, you only have to drive a few yards. It will be OK.'

My sister Maisie had come in to look at the filming that day, and she was amazed at how hard we worked. She couldn't believe what a serious grind of a job it was when I got into this car to try to drive those few yards.

The clutch has always been a problem to me, and try as I might I couldn't stop the car from jumping up and down as though it had a kangaroo under the bonnet instead of an engine. Out of the corner of my eye I could see our Maisie doubled up with laughter, and then I cracked up as well. I'll never know how we got that scene finished. When the girls got out they were all saying, 'Never again. We're never having a lift from you again.' And the crew were all in stitches.

If Jack was in the car scene with me it was a lot better, if a bit uncomfortable. Bill used to reach his right leg over me to operate the clutch, the pedal that always foxed me. That didn't work too badly but it sent Bill into contortions if he had a few lines to say as we drove off.

Once the factory girls had a trip to France – not that we got any further than Manchester for filming, I'm afraid. My heart sank when I read in the script that Vera wanted to learn some French. Then, as I read on, I realised I actually had to speak a line of French.

I always find English hard enough to learn. But French! It was just some line that meant 'The potatoes are in the dining room.' But there was no way I could learn to read French properly so I just had the words written down phonetically, and I tried to learn them parrot fashion. We all had a big laugh about Vera speaking French, and of course she wasn't supposed to have anything but a strong Weatherfield accent.

Then, just before the camera rehearsal, Johnny Briggs went and hid my book with the line written in it. It was only a joke, but I went mad. I started rooting through all this jeans material near my machine thinking that something had just got put on top of it. I had every-thing upside down and I finished up on my hands and knees on the floor desperately searching for the vital line. I was really beginning to panic, thinking, 'What will I say when it comes to me?'

Just before I fainted from fright Johnny grinned with that evil little grin of his and gave it back. I could have killed him. I said, 'You rotten sod.' It took me until a while later before I saw the joke.

He is a real old pro, Johnny. He has been around. We have had some great scenes together. We both miss the old factory where Mike Baldwin and Vera used to have such battles.

My memory is so bad that sometimes I don't know how I ever get my lines into my head. Once Sally Whit-taker, who plays little Sally Webster, came into the green room complaining about a car that was blocking the entrance to the car park.

She read out the licence number and asked us all if we knew anyone who had a car with that number. To help her get an answer I read out the number a bit louder, with some special Vera Duckworth volume. Everyone shook their heads and went back to their scripts, and then Sally said, 'But Liz, that's your car number.' And of course it was. I would forget my own head if it was loose.

I know it sounds a bit corny but the *Coronation Street* cast really are one great big happy family. I don't think we would ever get the show on the road if we weren't.

I enjoyed my scenes with my screen grandson Tommy when Terry's young wife Lisa, played by Caroline Milmoe, was giving birth in North Manchester hospital. It really reminded me of my times of giving birth. Not that that is something you ever forget. Caroline was a good laugh and she and I were experimenting a bit with the gas and air there for real mothers to be. I think we were just on the verge of getting a bit squiffy when we came to do the scene.

We had another funny time when we women of the Street had a party in the Rovers Return to sell saucy lingerie. That was just like the Pippa Dee Pantie Parties I used to organise to boost my housekeeping when Don and I were first married.

Every Monday another week starts and you have another three episodes of television to put together. That's an hour and a half a week, every week. It always staggers me, it's like a factory with one relentless production line that simply never stops.

We get on because we have to get on. We depend on each other. You can't survive for a long time in *Coronation Street* without fitting in as one of the team. I have great respect for every single one of the cast, but of course I am friendliest with the actor I work with the most, Bill Tarmey who plays my screen husband Jack Duckworth.

Bill is the only one of the cast that I regularly socialise with. He and his wife Ali often go out with Don and me. Sometimes that can be a bind because members of the public come up and start to think we are really married. It can get difficult for Don and Ali. They can get pushed aside.

It is the pace of the programme that eats you up. If you're working with a reasonable storyline it is all-consuming. You hardly have time to do anything else with your life.

We start a fresh week with our rehearsals on a Tuesday. That is when we go through a new week for the first time. We will have had that script for a week then, so as we start going through the scenes we are handed another three scripts for the following week. I often don't feel like looking at the new script until I've mastered the one we're working on, but I'm only human. I always find myself taking a look to see how many scenes we have.

One of the constant disappointments is the way our storylines seem to be leaked to newspapers so often. I know the viewers don't like to have their enjoyment spoiled in this way and I feel sorry for them. Of course no one knows who tells the Press what is going to happen in the future, but I think it's a great shame.

When you are being featured prominently in the story you often spend the weekend doing location filming. All the supermarket scenes, which I enjoyed when Vera was busy stacking shelves at Bettabuys, for instance, are recorded on a Sunday when the real supermarket that we use is closed to the public.

Sometimes it really feels like a treadmill. On Tuesday and Wednesday morning you have that ninety minutes of television to learn, and if you have a lot of scenes then you can be really up against it. I don't find it easy to get the lines into my head, and afterwards I can't remember any of them.

Wednesday afternoon is the technical run and we all feel we have to know our lines by then, that we have to give a real performance for the crew, the producer and everybody.

That's why we don't have time to talk much, apart from 'Hello, how are you?' Usually when you see two or three people talking they are deeply in character going through their lines. The weeks just fly by.

It takes your life over. Changing from two episodes a week to three changed my life. Vera was in demand, so often Saturday, Sunday and Monday were filming, Tuesday and Wednesday were rehearsing, and then Thursday and Friday were filming. And then you were often back on location again on Saturday.

It's incredible, but I am not really complaining. I believe the schedule is just something we must accept if we want to be in the best show in Britain. But the pressure can be very tough. We don't want to cause any ripples or let anyone down, so we buckle down and do it.

Lots of times I have got home at the end of the day and just sat in my car outside the house. My head would still be spinning from work and I have sat there thinking, 'I don't want to go in just yet. I just want to sit here without anyone telling me anything or asking me anything. I just want to cut off and not think about anything.'

I believe Vera is a very popular character and I think the writers like to write for her. That's great, but sometimes it means that the workload can be very, very hard. But nobody complains about being given too much work – the alternative is not too attractive a prospect.

When I first got into *Coronation Street* it wasn't the fame that bothered me, it was the money. You see, I was living in a council house – not that there is anything wrong with council houses, sometimes I feel I would be much happier if I had stayed in one – with four young kids and a husband to look after. The sort of money the *Street* paid was at the same time desperately needed and beyond my wildest dreams. I honestly never had any serious ambitions of becoming a real actress. I was just a young mum struggling to feed her family and make the best of herself.

As I started in the *Street* on my short-term arrangements I used to go straight to the bank manager and say, 'Hey, I want a loan. I've got that six-week contract.' But although they keep using me quite a bit and asking me back it was always three weeks here and six weeks there.

In those early days the money was marvellous but it came in small chunks. All the time I would be thinking, 'I could finish tomorrow and I would be back working in a real factory.'

I suppose it's easier if you haven't got a family but if you have a family you will always have someone to love and to care about, and I think that is everything.

I get all the attention in our family, but really my sister Maisie is the remarkable one. She has done really well in life and after leaving school she went back into education and became a lecturer. Now she is in charge of a business studies department at a college in Leeds.

She also became a councillor on West Yorkshire Metropolitan County Council. I campaigned for her. I stood outside the booth and I stuck Maisie's stickers on everyone, even the Conservatives. One chap got really awkward and snorted, 'I don't vote Labour, take that off.' I said, 'I won't.' I must admit Maisie couldn't decide whether I was helping or not. She told me I was just supposed to give them to her supporters, but that seemed a bit tame for me so I decided to go all out and get some new recruits. I decided there wasn't that much difference between show business and politics.

Maisie was terrified that the vote would be declared null and void or whatever because I had swung the balance unfairly. And it was very close when she got in. I must admit that when young kids came running up for autographs I used to tell them to go and get their mother to vote for Maisie before I would sign. I think that's what politics needs, a bit of razzmatazz.

Maisie calls it my illusion that really I would have liked to have been a little housewife and just stayed at home, baking bread and looking after the children. It doesn't seem like an illusion to me, but maybe she's right. If I'm honest I hate baking, I don't really like cooking at all.

I often feel tired, but I find rest hard to take. When I get time off work I find I'm always doing things. If I have one quality that has kept me going, it is a sort of energy – my drive, I call it – but it's always kept me going through thick and thin. I have never really been happy with the status quo. I pack my diary with things to do.

I always wanted more. That is why I let Don encourage me into singing, that's why I did Avon, sold wigs, held Tupperware parties and all those other crazy things. I was never quite satisfied with sitting back and enjoying what we had. I wanted to push on and do more, achieve more, and have more.

My sister always says it's modesty when I say I don't know how I came to be here, starring in *Coronation Street*. She tells me I'm the most self-deprecating person she has ever known, that I put myself down all the time. She says I do have talent and that although I have been lucky I have worked very hard to capitalise on that good fortune.

All the same, I do feel uncomfortable making so much money when some people have so little. Because I have been hard up I know what it feels like. When I see a young mother walking along in winter still wearing her thin summer clothes, I really feel for her because I've been there. I know what it's like not to be able to afford a nice warm coat, and it's not a nice feeling.

I suppose in a way my whole life has been preparing me for success, for life as *Coronation Street's* Vera

Duckworth. All the way through I have done things that have led to something else, but it has always been built upon a foundation of hard work. I trailed up and down the country doing the clubs for years before I got a break with Cadbury's Cookies. That was my apprenticeship.

Happiness, I have learned, has nothing to do with how much money you have got or how big a house you live in. We're all who we are underneath. We all act and hide things, hide who we are and how we really feel. We all feel annoyed at some time or another and have to hide it.

My job is my life. I play Vera all day and then I come home and have two hours of trying to be myself before I come downstairs and start learning my lines and becoming Vera again.

Not that it's nice every time you appear on television. One of my show business regrets is letting my home be featured on the quiz show *Through the Keyhole*.

I like watching the show, so I said yes without really thinking about it. We had only been in the house a few months. The house had suffered a fire and been rebuilt as new, and when we moved in it had been empty for six years. There were no carpets, no curtains and no fittings for anything either. It was just a bare shell.

I had been frantically busy at work. We had had a wedding to arrange because our daughter Anne had come home from Italy very much in love with her Italian boyfriend. We had rushed to get the house carpeted and curtained as quickly as possible. We bought a huge roll of carpet and for the sake of speed we had the same thing all the way through the house.

It was all green, and it made the inside of the house look like a huge tennis court. And Don went down to a curtain wholesalers and we got fitted throughout as quickly as possible because we wanted to get the house ready for all these people coming over from Italy for the wedding. It was the worst possible time to choose to go on *Through the Keyhole*. I must have been mad, but 'no' is always a word I find hard to come out with.

I didn't understand that sometimes they pulled houses to bits. Pattie Caldwell really had a go at my house. Yorkshire TV did edit some of the nastiest remarks out but she still said things, like there were no flowers in the garden, but we hadn't been there long enough for them to grow! I felt very uncomfortable because for that show you have to sit in the studio in Leeds listening to whatever they want to dish up. I should have known it was not going to go well because I forgot my wig – I left it on top of the wardrobe. So I didn't even feel right. However, Patrick Litchfield said he really liked my bedroom, so at least something met with approval.

One person I never met was Marti Caine. I often followed her into clubs and of course I knew about her. But one night my son came home and said, 'I've got Marti Caine's autograph.' He had it written on a tiny piece of paper no bigger than my thumbnail. I said, 'Do you mean you asked her to sign that miserable scrap of paper?' He said, 'Yes. And I told her my mother was in *Coronation Street*.' She said, 'She must be either Lynne Perrie or Liz Dawn.'

If you do three episodes of *Coronation Street* and you're outside filming, you might not get a day off. And every week brings another three episodes. It's not like working in a factory where you can do the job with your eyes shut. Each director has their own way of working and their individual creative vision.

Bill and I have a good timing working together, and that takes years to build up. We make each other laugh on screen as well as off. We have never had a row. I think I have given him a few headaches because I talk a lot.

We have a lot in common. We come from the same background, having made it up through the clubs. Although that is good experience in one way and it certainly does give you confidence and the ability to ad-lib and work an audience, it can be a very solo life as a singer like I was. It is just down to you when you're out there on stage. It's a challenge to entertain that audience. Coming from that background to the very different world of television where it is very much a team effort that produces the best results takes quite a lot of getting used to.

The audience is just as vital to *Coronation Street* as it is in the clubs, but you are communicating in a totally different way and you have to work as a team with other actors, writers, the director, the cameraman, the sound man, make-up, wardrobe. All these people have an important role to play, and *Coronation Street* only works as well as it does because all these people work well together. I understand this now, but when I first got there I didn't.

I know now that when I first went into the *Street* I unknowingly did my cabaret act a bit. I wanted to show all these experienced actors that I could do it, so I put on a bit of a front as you might say. All the excellent actors and actresses who had been formally trained at drama school must have thought, 'Who the hell's this?' There is a feeling that the 'turns' are one groups and the 'luvvies' are another. You have to blend in. In the early days we all used to mix in and share dressing rooms. But directors used to say to me, 'You didn't need teaching. You didn't need to go to drama school. You have got it.'

The *Street* has brought the most incredible people into my life. I met Dustin Hoffman at the premier of *Tootsie* in Manchester, and he was really nice. I was so nervous, I felt just like a fan. People are always asking me for my autograph and I felt like asking him for his.

We talked about the different things that make people laugh in Britain and in America. He was lovely and down to earth. But as he had just been playing *Tootsie* and doing so well to look like a woman I thought he might be looking at me and thinking, 'That is not her own hair.'

Shouting has got on my nerves over the years. Can you imagine going to work and then yelling all day?

Lately I have been trying to get Vera to speak a bit more quietly, but the director always asks for a bit more of Vera's volume. Sometimes I say, 'Do I have to shout all the time?' I have got a loud voice.

Three years ago I even went for elocution lessons. Can you believe that? I went to a lovely woman called Edith just round the corner from where I live in Manchester.

I had been thinking to myself that if ever I was written out of *Coronation Street* there was no way I would get a part in anything else because of my voice. It's so like Vera's and I've never had any training as to how to change it.

So I thought if I learned to speak proper I might be all right. Edith is a really lovely woman, and for a while I progressed at the voice exercises and began to sound like a minor member of the Royal Family. My daughters began to object to me declaiming all over the house. And it was hard to fit it in with all the work in the *Street*.

One night I forgot I had a lesson and when I got home from Granada Don reminded me I was booked for a session with Edith. I dashed round there without thinking and then I was worried that I hadn't practised the exercise she had set me.

So I went in, talking as posh as I could, and I just about kept a conversation going until I tripped and fell flat out on the settee. Suddenly I forgot my snooty voice and came out with, 'My God, I'm knackered,' in pure Vera Duckworth. Edith laughed but I think we both

realised we had come to the end of my elocution lessons.
I just couldn't find the time or the energy to follow them
through any more.

Soon afterwards the morning television show *The
Time, The Place* did a programme on accents, and I went
on with Edith. But I made a complete idiot of myself. I
couldn't do the different voices very well. If I really
wanted to go upmarket or join the Royal Shakespeare
Company I would have to have Edith with me twenty-
four hours a day.

Sometimes I think, Should I go on? When people
ask me I always come out with the same jokey answer
that I want to go on as long as Ena Sharples and then
drop dead in the Rovers, but underneath I am not so sure
that is really how I feel. I think, Well, do I want that?
Because the things I've missed are so important.

The truth is that people don't realise what it is like
being a regular on *Coronation Street*. How could they?
The viewers don't know how much work goes into it
week after week. The things you can't do because of it!

When *EastEnders* started becoming successful, I
cheered, because I thought, Great. Let us share this pressure of being in a top soap with someone else. We're like
Charles and Di. We sell newspapers – but at least we're
not bugged.

My kids have never come home to an empty house.
Although I was working and trying to be a singer and an
actress when they were little I always had family and
friends who would help out.

During the week I always used to be there to pick them up from school, but at the weekend when most families went out together I would be singing, so it did fit in with our lives in a way.

It is interesting with this baby in the *Street* with Tommy. It has brought a lot of memories back for me. My four children each have their own thoughts on my life. Often the programme has interfered with the family and when they have seen me full of stress over lines or general pressure they have all said from time to time, 'Oh mother, why don't you pack it in?'

The truth is, I'm not sure I would know what to do without Vera. She has brought me such a lot of fun as well as everything else. The one person who spotted the essence of Vera and copied it so brilliantly was impressionist Dustin Gee. He was a very talented young comic and I always loved his affectionate impersonations.

I first met Dustin long before either of us had made it into the public eye. By coincidence we once shared a railway compartment on a journey in the North of England to club dates. We introduced ourselves and found we had lots of friends in common. He finished up sharing my flask of coffee and making the trip flash quickly by.

The next time he registered with me was when he and Les Dennis first did that wickedly funny impression of Mavis Riley and Vera. Both Thelma Barlow, who plays Mavis so wonderfully well, and I saw the joke from the start.

We were very flattered to be taken off so beautifully, and we met up from time to time with Les and Dustin. The best time was when I was sneaked into the Bradford Alhambra to surprise them on stage in pantomime.

They were playing the ugly sisters and as I crept up behind them the audience went wild when they spotted me, long before Dustin realised, approaching this rude rival of the curly wig. He had the line, 'Well, I don't know what I'm going to do now,' and I finished it off by interrupting with, 'Well, I do,' and Dustin was really staggered.

Russ Abbot, who was the star of the show, thought it was a huge joke, but I managed to surprise him with a special showbiz award presentation from Yorkshire Television at the end of the evening. We had a marvellous night together.

It was tragic when Dustin died so young. He was only forty-three when he passed away in 1985. Of course I went to his funeral in York, which turned out to be just the sort of amusing, uplifting affair Dustin would have loved. He was in pantomime in *Snow White and the Seven Dwarfs* in Southport when he died, and the dwarfs came and carried his coffin at the funeral. It looked so funny, floating along low down as if by magic. I know he would have approved, and it was a moving tribute from his fellow artists.

I do wish they would bring the factory back. We always had such a laugh. Once the script had the girls all ganging up on poor old Ernie Bishop and stripping him of his trousers, and we had a scream doing that scene. Stephen Hancock who played Ernie had stuffed something unmentionable down his trousers to give us a fright so we had to have quite a lot of rehearsals. I liked Stephen, but he left when Ernie Bishop was shot in an armed robbery at the factory. That was one of the *Street's* very few violent scenes, it was sensational.

Being in *Coronation Street* is not a normal life. Playing the part of another person, day in day out, for nineteen years is not exactly a normal thing to do. Everyone thinks they know you. In Kendal's they say, 'Eh, is it true you're chucking Jack out?' I say, 'I'll be the last to know,' but I think it is so ridiculous to find yourself having long, involved conversations about this imaginary person called Vera who everyone knows so well.

If you worked in a factory and you were ill or your children were ill and you couldn't come in, then they would put someone else on your job, but you couldn't put a curly wig on somebody else and say, 'Play Vera Duckworth,' and that is where the strain comes in.

The danger of appearing on something like *Coronation Street* is that it can distance you from ordinary people. It can make people think that you are somehow special and different from them. I love to go out and meet people and have a laugh with them and show them that I'm real. But the things ordinary people do all the time are not so easy if you're in a soap opera.

Hundreds of times I have been to work when I've

been feeling less than 100 per cent – in fact some times I have felt suicidal as I have driven there. But just as I approach the gates, I don't know what happens to me, I always smile at the security men and wave, when even two minutes before I've been feeling really fed up. The acting starts before the acting starts, if you know what I mean. I am acting as I go in and start meeting people.

We're all like that. We have all got different pressures upon us. The great thing is that I get on very well with Bill, he is genuinely such a nice guy. When he had his heart operation it was awful. His wonderful 'real' wife Ali was a tower of strength. Thank God he recovered from that and is still my Jack.

When people ask you about the *Street* your automatic reaction is to say how wonderful it is, and there is a lot of warmth that you get from people. But sometimes I really wish I was as anonymous as the next face in the bus queue.

The success of the *Street* is down to the viewers, the ordinary man and woman in the street, and to them I am Vera Duckworth, not an actress at all, but a loud woman with a curly wig who comes into their homes three times a week.

Sometimes you can get a bit of an identity crisis – start wondering who you are, Vera or Liz, or Sylvia come to that. When I was very down I once went to a woman my sister recommended, a famous psychiatrist.

It was after an operation and I was all of a dither. After an op the anaesthetic can do funny things to you, and I was in a terrible state. I wanted to pack everything in and go back to live in Leeds.

I went in and the only two words the psychiatrist got out were, 'Sit down.' I never shut up. I started with, 'I found my granny dead. I was the first one they told that my mother had cancer. The doctor ran after me and said, "Can I have a word? Your mother has only got three to six months." I found my dad dead in bed because I went the wrong way into the hospital.' I just blurted it all out. I couldn't stop, and this woman was a bit taken aback. After a while I ran out of steam and said, 'Well, I feel better now,' and she still had not spoken. Later she said to Maisie, 'Your sister could have had a breakdown at any time in the last seven years.'

When they got me for *This Is Your Life* I was waiting to go into hospital for an operation, so I was hardly feeling my best. The programme was in October, and I went in for the operation in December. I put my operation off three times because of the demands of *Street* storylines.

I had my eyes done at the same time. It was great to get all those horrible lines removed, I felt so much better afterwards. I came out with two black eyes but I felt a lot better. Eyes are special to women. The skin around there is one of those areas that seems to be the first to go. It is the bit of your face that shows all your tiredness.

I said to the surgeon who was doing the operation, 'I just want to look less tired.' I wanted those bags under my eyes unpacking for a while. They looked as though they were ready for a round-the-world trip when I went in. I didn't want anything drastic. I never regretted it. Since then I have met lots of women who go on and on about all the wrinkles round their eyes. I always say, 'Get them done. You'll feel a lot better.' You can have the operation and go out the same day.

I don't see anything wrong with a bit of cosmetic surgery here and there to keep you looking your best. Some women save up and have a new three-piece suite. I would rather make do with the old suite and be happier with what I could see in the mirror. Anyway it's very common now. I saved up to get my eyes done, and I've never looked back! I hope you'll excuse the dreadful pun.

But that was why I was hardly looking my best when Michael Aspel approached me with that big red book. I felt so down and weak.

Don dropped me off in town that morning. He had to go to Granada, and I went shopping. He had been behaving so strangely with all the preparations that I had started to suspect he had another woman. He seemed to be putting the phone down on some mysterious call every time I walked in the room.

They had told me I was required to do a promotional programme about the *Street* for Canada. They had offered to send a car for me, and that was the only thing I thought was a bit odd. When they realised I had gone off shopping they started to panic that I would turn up too soon while they were still setting up the catch, because Bill Tarmey who knows me pretty well said, 'She's liable to just jump in a taxi and turn up.' They had people following me round Kendal's. I was there ambling around the lingerie department and they had a couple of women following me radioing back about my whereabouts.

They must have been good at shadowing because I never knew. Don had liaised with the researchers all the way through and I never smelt a rat.

As it happens I arrived at the studio on time. I was really a bit put out to be dragged in on one of my days off to do this thing for Canada. I was feeling a bit down and I had a little cry in my dressing room. The wardrobe lady came in and asked me what the matter was. I said, 'I am just so tired. Why have I had to come in on my day off?'

Then in the scene where they 'caught' me it seemed strange because I had to shout 'Jack' when he wasn't even in the Rovers. I said, 'How can he hear me through the doors?' and they assured me they would time it so he was just coming in.

I had made six *This Is Your Life* appearances as a guest before, so I knew the format pretty well. It would have felt completely different if I had never been on one. I knew exactly about the spot on the stage where people had to stand, and how Michael kept it all going so well. Once I had been surprised, which was a big shock, I wanted everything to run smoothly. I knew my children were coming on and I wanted to make it as easy as possible for them while I still didn't want to make a fool of myself.

I knew that my family and friends would have all had a really long day because television studios can be very hot and boring places when you're being ordered about through all the endless rehearsals. I was worried about my daughter-in-law with her baby, and it was actually my grandson Thomas's birthday that day.

I was so worried about how everyone else was feeling that when Don's voice was booming behind the screens I didn't recognise it at first. Michael Aspel looked really worried for a minute. I think he was wondering if the researchers had got the wrong man!

It was wonderful to see all my family and friends together. Nearly all the cast were there and even people who weren't in it at the time, like Nigel Pivaro who plays my screen son Terry. I was delighted he had made it. The producers liked it because there was a big family to be the centre of it all.

Bernard Manning gave a tribute to me, which was nice, even if he did call me a Lancashire lass instead of Yorkshire. Maybe Vera sounded so Lancashire that had convinced him.

It is a terrific honour because they only ever do so many of them. I just wish I had felt healthier while it was happening. I was on my last legs when I did it.

Vera has got me into some amazing places. I've really enjoyed cruises on the *QE2*. On one voyage I did a radio interview with Liz Kershaw. We were sitting chatting in the captain's cabin and she said, 'Liz, did you know that one couple have paid £5,000 to come and see you on this ship? How do you feel about that?'

I said, 'Tell them they could have come and had a tour round my back bedroom for £400!' It's hard to take that sort of thing seriously, to realize just how much *Street* characters mean to people. It makes you very proud and grateful.

Flying over to Canada first class was a real treat as well. Bill and his wife came with us to meet some of the Canadian fans, who really love the *Street*. It's on five nights a week in Canada now and doing very well.

The country was absolutely stunning, but freezing cold. Every time you went outside the air was so cold it was like being stung. A firm gave us Hudson Bay coats, complete with big furry hats. We went to an amazing ice exhibition and round their Parliament building. We were treated like royalty, they were so kind.

I met Margaret Thatcher when she came to the *Street*. I think she's the best actress I've ever met. My sister Maisie threatened never to speak to me again, but I met her all the same.

I met the Queen when she came round *Coronation Street*. But it was hardly my greatest moment.

The Queen said to me, 'The factory has not always been here, has it?' I was so stunned I couldn't speak. I suddenly felt like Harpo Marx in that curly wig, totally dumbstruck. It was remarkable enough meeting the Queen, but having her actually speak to me and ask me a question was just too much. My mind raced back to my granny and her pictures of my Uncle Joe in the ranks behind the Queen on the Royal Yacht *Britannia*. I thought of how proud she, and my mother, would have been to think that little Sylvia Butterfield was meeting the Queen. All that went through my head in a rush.

Helen Palmer, who was standing next to me, was terribly quiet as well. Johnny Briggs smiled and said, 'Ma'am, I've never known these two be so quiet.' And we all laughed.

Suddenly Sir Denis Foreman, one of the founding fathers of Granada, stepped forward and the Queen turned to him and said, 'I've just been saying, the factory has not always been here.'

We watched it later on the news. The newsreader said, 'Now here is the Queen meeting Liz Dawn, better known as Vera Duckworth, I'm sorry, I mean Vera Duckworth, better known as Liz Dawn.' I just couldn't believe the whole experience. The Queen discussing where Mike Baldwin's factory used to be! Maybe *Coronation Street* is real life after all.

The Royal Variety in 1989 was one of the highlights of my career, but I'm afraid I remember it for hitting the headlines for all the wrong reasons.

We were all down at the London Palladium to do a Rover's Return sketch. It was really funny and we were all very pleased to be there. Sometimes in shows like the Royal Variety series like *Coronation Street* miss out on the limelight. They tend to concentrate more on individual performers, but this was one time we really got our chance.

Unfortunately during the rehearsals I got myself in

a real twist when I was being fitted with my stage microphone. The chap who wired me up left my dress tucked into my knickers at the back so I almost brought the house down with an impromptu strip show.

I felt a draught and wondered why I could hear all these people giggling. Jill Summers, who plays Phyllis Pearce, helped me out of my embarrassment when she told me what happened. I could have died. I was just pleased that it was only a run through. If the Queen and the Duke of Edinburgh had seen it happen I would never have lived it down. I'm not exactly the smallest person. Prince Philip would have taken one look and said, 'What's that?' As it was I managed to grab all the publicity. I don't suppose anyone believed it was an accident, but it most certainly was.

Jill Summers is quite a character. She was a big star years ago, and now she is in her eighties she still is. I have enormous respect for her. But sometimes that presents a problem. When Vera was battling to get baby Tommy from Des Barnes after poor Lisa was knocked down and killed by a car outside the Rovers, Jill and I had one scene together that I found really difficult.

Phyllis was baby-sitting at Des's house when I had to go round there and I was supposed to get really angry and shout, 'What on earth are you doing here?' at Jill. In the script it said I had to really yell and carry on, but it just didn't feel right. I said to the director, 'I'm not going to shout at Jill. I've got too much respect for her.'

They both said, 'But it's acting,' and we all fell

about laughing. Sometimes you get so involved in it all you forget what day it is, let alone what's real and what is acting.

I first met Jill when I was about twenty-six. She was the star of a big charity night for UNICEF at a place in Wakefield. She was really nice to everyone. I was just somebody way down the bill singing a couple of songs and she was the big name, but she couldn't have been kinder.

I met Prince Charles at the Prince of Wales Hospice. He wanted to be involved in a hospice from start to finish. He was really charming. I said to him, 'You're my favourite Royal.' But he just smiled and said, 'It won't get you anywhere.' I wanted to take a photograph but apparently protocol doesn't allow them to be photographed when they are drinking. It was only orange juice, but he said, 'I'll put my glass down,' and the snap was taken.

Afterwards a waitress said, 'Would you like Prince Charles's orange juice?' and I knocked it back. So you could say the heir to the throne and I have shared a drink. It did cross my mind to put the glass in my bag and give it pride of place on the Duckworths' bar but I thought better of it and handed it back.

I am an enormous fan of the Royals. I know it's not very fashionable to say that these days, but I don't care. I think they work very hard for the country and do a grand job. The day I met Prince Charles he was going on to do another three jobs. Not all of those get reported in the papers. I don't think the Royal Family is to blame for the state of the country, but that's another story.

I've only ever known two celebrities sit on the Duckworths' set to be filmed – Cilla Black and Michael Aspel. Cilla came up to Granada to do a tribute programme to the *Street*. When she came into the set of No. 9 and sat on the Duckworths' sofa it was covered in dust. I felt so embarrassed as if it really was Vera's responsibility to keep it clean. But Cilla was marvellous, so warm and friendly. We really got on. I could see her husband Bobby in the background, and I shouted to him to come on. Afterwards she asked for that piece of videotape.

Michael Aspel must be a good actor. Bill's *This Is Your Life* was filmed in the Duckworths' and I had to do an impromptu scene with him. I think it was the quickest piece of filming I've ever done. Michael surprised Bill in the Rovers, but as they took him away to get ready for the studio show they wanted a bit more footage of Michael on the Street.

So he came into No. 9 and we just made it up as we went along. It was the weirdest thing I've ever done because it seemed so natural, me as Vera asking Michael to sit down and have a cup of tea. He must be a good actor.

13
Here's to the Future

After almost twenty years of playing Vera Duckworth I think I know the lady pretty well. She is loud, proud, and full of life. She has had her highs and her lows, but her strength of character pulls her through every crisis.

I am delighted that the viewers seem to like her and enjoy watching her so much. The outside of our set is open to the public within the very successful Granada Studios Tour. I think it is smashing that viewers can actually walk down Coronation Street and see it for themselves. I know it means a lot to many of them.

It means a lot to me that they often linger outside No. 9, my happy home. Tour guides tell me that the most enthusiastic fans even try to prise off a little scrap of Vera's wonderful stone cladding as a souvenir. And our doorknob went missing in highly suspicious circumstances years ago!

I don't mind because I think it means that Jack and Vera have really made it with the viewers. I was delighted when a top-selling magazine wrote to tell me that a readers' poll had voted the Duckworths as the 'neighbours you would least like to live next door to'.

I know it's a bit of a back-handed compliment, but I

think it means that Bill Tarmey and I are doing our job if we still provoke that reaction. For the future, I would be proud and pleased to carry on as long as *Coronation Street* continues. Here's to the next twenty years!